WITCHES
THEN & NOW

Inside Their Mysterious World

EDITED BY SHARI GOLDHAGEN

CENTENNIAL BOOKS

WITCHES
THEN & NOW
Inside Their Mysterious World

CONTENTS

10

84

90

142

THE WORLD.

WELCOME
TO THE
WITCH

*The mysterious figure is one of humanity's oldest archetypes,
but the symbol still resonates today with new relevance.*

Revelers in the forest celebrating solstice with a dance.
*A wrinkled crone tossing eye of newt into a cauldron.
Feminists in pointy black hats marching for social justice.
An enchantress in a slinky dress.
Midwives and healers.
Teenage outcasts finding their voice.
Broomstick riders.
Liberated ladies.
Readers of tea leaves and tarot cards.
Someone who challenges the status quo.*

Ask 10 people what a witch is, and it's possible to get 10 different answers. Yet everyone is familiar with the concept.

It's not a stretch to say the idea of the witch is as old as recorded history. Going back thousands of years, in almost every culture, you'll find tales— fact and fiction—of people (usually women) with suspected magical powers. Sometimes witches have been sought out and celebrated for their abilities, like renowned fortune teller Mother Shipton. Sadly, many who have been labeled witches have been shunned, or worse, for not conforming to societal norms (during the witch hunts, the accused were often women who had sex outside of marriage or didn't attend church).

While there may be countless images of the witch, all those incarnations have one thing in common: The witch almost always has agency and drives the action.

"A witch is someone who is in touch with her power," says Sandra Ramos, an activist also known as the Purple Lady in the woods. "A witch doesn't let society dictate what she can do."

That might explain why witches, far from being old (pointy black) hat, still fascinate and inspire after 4,000 years.

Their legacy continues to play a major role in our collective consciousness and shared stories, whether it's Anne Hathaway's remake of *The Witches* or *Cursed*, Netflix's twist on the Arthurian legend focused on the Lady of the Lake.

With their emphasis on nature and the Earth, pagan religions are some of the fastest-growing faiths in the world. And witches have become a symbol for those who stand up against oppressive societies.

"The witch is the ultimate archetype for anyone who wants to find power outside of patriarchal systems," says Pam Grossman, author of *Waking the Witch* and host of the podcast The Witch Wave. "Anyone who is drawn to her is aligning themselves with independence and freedom and self-sovereignty. The word witch is available to anyone who feels drawn to it."

Welcome.   *—Shari Goldhagen*

CHAPTER 1

A BEWITCHING HISTORY

EXPLORE THE EVOLUTION OF THE WITCH ACROSS CULTURES, FROM ANCIENT ORIGINS TO MODERN MAGIC. READ ABOUT THE SAD STORY OF THE WITCH HUNTS IN THE WESTERN WORLD, AND MEET SOME OF THE CRAFT'S MOST FAMOUS FACES, INCLUDING MARIE LAVEAU AND MOTHER SHIPTON.

A *Spellbinding* Journey

Whether feared or exalted, witches have been a part of nearly every society since humans began keeping records.

Julius Kronberg's "Hypatia" shows the scholar at work, with a nervous eye on the temple outside.

Hypatia of Alexandria wasn't your average fifth-century woman. Trained by her father in mathematics, philosophy and astronomy, she was a respected academic, something reserved for men at the time. Crowds would gather to hear her speak of Plato and Aristotle, ideas that didn't sit well with Christians in the region. She was also a practicing pagan, though she believed in religious tolerance for all. Decried as a witch, a mob primarily made up of Christian monks pulled her from her chariot as she was leaving the university in A.D. 415. The group stripped, brutally beat and burned her to death; all of her academic work was destroyed.

It's one of the first documented instances of an accused witch being murdered, but the phenomenon itself was nothing new. Humans have been worrying about witches for more than 4,000 years. "In every inhabited continent of the world, the majority of recorded human societies have believed in and feared an ability by some individuals to cause misfortune and injury to others by nonphysical and uncanny (magical) means," writes Ronald Hutton, PhD, in *The Witch: A History of Fear, From Ancient Times to the Present.*

More often than not, these witches were, like Hypatia, people living outside societal norms in one way or another. And though both men and women have practiced all sorts of magic, or been accused of having done so, the vast majority of fear and loathing has been directed at women.

"The feminine has so often been reviled or undervalued throughout history," says Pam Grossman, author of *Waking the Witch* and host of The Witch Wave podcast. "Anytime there is a powerful woman or person who is outside that patriarchal status quo, they

AN OWL OR THE STRIX?

are going to be framed as unruly and potentially dangerous."

ANCIENT WITCH-STORY

The witch can be found in Judaic traditions in the Old Testament's Book of Samuel (written between 931 and 721 B.C.). Despite having banned the craft, King Saul, who was at war with the Philistines, disguises himself and asks a woman known as the Witch of Endor to summon the prophet Samuel for advice. After some protesting, she complies and,

John William Waterhouse's "Circe Invidiosa" shows the witch goddess poisoning the water where Scylla bathes, creating a monster.

Adam's first wife contemplates her beauty in Dante Gabriel Rossetti's "Lady Lilith."

"THE WITCH IS THE PERFECT SYMBOL FOR ANYONE WHO WANTS TO CHALLENGE PATRIARCHAL OR OPPRESSIVE SYSTEMS."

❧ *Pam Grossman*

through the prophet, sees Saul and his sons will die. The lads are killed in battle the next day and Saul dies by suicide—fulfilling her vision.

Depending on the faith, the story has conflicting meanings, but the Bible explicitly gives witches the thumbs-down in Exodus 22:18, which states, "Thou shalt not suffer a witch to live." And then there's Lilith, Adam's first wife (first mentioned around the third to fifth century), who was kicked out of Eden for disobedience. Some stories see her becoming something of a witch known to eat children.

Eating kids, it turns out, was apparently a favored pastime of ancient-culture witches. More often than not, these tot nibblers were old, childless hags. Roman lore offers tales of the Strix, a night owl who could assume the form of a human woman and would fly around gobbling up kiddies. She's thought to have been an influence in the Slavic tales of the child-eating Baba Yaga.

Greek stories have the similarly aerial-loving Lamia, who sucks the blood of young men following the deaths of her own children. And the Roman poet Horace wrote of the Witch Canidia, who was a real woman, although tales of how she practiced blood sacrifices and starved small boys are thought to be fabricated.

Not all practitioners of magic were straight-up evil. Greek and Roman mythology depicts witches using spells for good, or at least morally ambivalent, purposes. In "The Odyssey" and *The Voyage of Argo*—texts dating back to the eighth century B.C.—Circe and Medea aid the mortal heroes Odysseus and Jason, even if love may have been a motivator.

In the Americas, witchcraft—both good and evil—was part of the Diné people's culture. Healers used powers to aid the community, but the Navajos also had a concept for harmful, witchlike individuals known as *yee nahgloshii* or skin-walkers, who could turn themselves into animals. Often they were highly trained medicine men who turned to the dark side and were initiated into a secret society after committing a nefarious act such as murdering a sibling.

In some Middle Eastern cultures, where powerful female deities were worshipped, wise women were trained in holy rituals. "They are so clearly understood to be positive figures in their society," biblical scholar Carole Fontaine, MAR, PhD, has said. "No king could be without their counsel, no army could recover from a defeat without their ritual activity, no baby could be born without their presence."

As in many ancient civilizations, sorcery and ghost culture in China served as a spiritual refuge for some—a way to explain the unexplainable. But as is often the case, witches were also used as scapegoats. In 91 B.C., aged Emperor Wudi believed his long illness

LAW CODE STELE OF KING HAMMURABI

was the work of witchcraft and brought in foreign shamans to help root out those using harmful magic. No one was above accusation; among those found guilty was Crown Prince Liu Ju, whose rooms were said to contain carvings of his victims, according to *BBC History*. The prince hanged himself following the discovery. Later, in the first century, multiple consorts to the emperor were denounced as witches. This idea of people practicing "gu" or harmful magic continued through medieval times.

EUROPE'S CRUEL CRAZE

All the way back in 1754 B.C., Hammurabi's Code in Babylon had passages about punishing those casting unjustified spells. And Rome's Lex Cornelia began forbidding various types of sorcery by 81 B.C. In Lex Salica, a Germanic code of laws assembled by Frankish King Clovis around A.D. 500, there was a fine of 200 solidi for each man a Stria (remember the Strix?) magically consumed, claims historian Max Dashu.

Despite these laws, it wasn't uncommon for people—especially those in rural villages—to seek a vision or herbal cure from a self-professed local witch. There were occasional accusations of evil magic in the Middle Ages, but punishments were largely doled out through mob action. In 1090, for example, three Bavarian peasant women were burned to death by neighbors claiming the trio had poisoned people and destroyed crops.

Things changed dramatically in the 15th century, when the church officially recognized witchcraft. As opposed to someone who may have been led astray by magic, the concept of the witch evolved to mean someone who had made a pact to serve Satan and harm Christians in exchange for otherworldly powers.

Witches proved easy targets for leaders at a loss to explain years of plague and famine rattling Europe. And according to economists Peter Leeson, PhD, and Jacob Russ, PhD, competition between the Catholic and newly formed

After falling in love with Jason, Medea used her witchcraft to help him steal the golden fleece from her father.

Protestant churches led the drive. "Similar to...contemporary Republican and Democratic candidates...historical Catholic and Protestant officials focused witch-trial activity in confessional battlegrounds...to attract loyalty of undecided Christians," they wrote in the *Economic Journal*.

It wasn't only the church. State officials were often deeply embroiled as well. King James VI Stuart of Scotland (later King James I of England) was an anti-witch zealot who personally questioned accused women, overseeing their torture.

In 1486, German clergyman Heinrich Kramer published *Malleus Maleficarum*, translated to *The Hammer of Witches* (the Rev. Jacob Sprenger's name was added to later editions). The book explicitly labeled witchcraft heresy and served as a guide to find and interrogate suspects. It became a popular tool for the church, which began a "great hunt" of witches in the 1500s.

Malleus Maleficarum was deeply misogynistic, with lines like, "When a woman thinks alone, she thinks evil." And it was particularly harsh on previously exalted female healers, claiming, "No one does more harm to the Catholic church than midwives."

Given that, it was hardly surprising the vast majority of those targeted during the witch hunts were poor, single women, who happened to be out of step with patriarchal systems of the time, claim Barbara Ehrenreich and Deirdre English in *Witches, Midwives, & Nurses*. "First, witches are accused of every conceivable sexual crime against men. Quite simply, they are 'accused' of female sexuality. Second, they are accused of being organized. Third, they are accused of having magical powers affecting health—of harming but also healing. They were often charged specifically for possessing medical and obstetrical skills."

To extract "confessions," investigators used all methods of torture, including sleep deprivation and sexual humiliation. Evidence against the accused could be as simple as having a "witch's mark," any unsightly blemish (which was often found while being publicly stripped), or failing a swim test by *not* drowning after being bound and thrown into a body of water. (It was thought a witch would float, because water would reject her body as she'd spurned baptism.) As many as 80,000 accused witches were put to death from 1500 to 1700 in Europe, and an estimated 75% to 85% of them were women.

German settlements were particularly barbaric, accounting for an estimated 25,000 executions. The territory of St. Maximin had only 2,200 residents, but by the mid-1500s, they'd executed more than 500 people. Among them: a woman named Eva, who confessed to murdering

> **"IN SOCIETIES WHERE...AGGRESSION AND RESENTMENT IS REPRESSED...THE WITCH...PROVIDED A...HUMAN BEING WHOM IT WAS NOT ONLY PROPER BUT NECESSARY TO HATE."**
>
> ❧ *Ronald Hutton, PhD*

a child via magic. In Bamberg, meanwhile, nearly 1,000 people were tortured and burned in crematoriums (to save firewood) between 1623 and 1631. Emperor Ferdinand finally issued a mandate to end the trials.

NEW WORLD, SAME SITCH

Europe's great hunt extended into the Americas as well. The Spanish, in particular, were keen on pushing Catholicism in the New World, Helen Pugh, author of *Intrepid Dudettes of the Inca Empire*, says. "This made them go on witch hunts to stamp out 'paganism.' Even more so when Protestantism began to emerge in Europe, they wanted to ensure the Catholicism of their subjects overseas."

In South America, an Inca princess named Quispe Sisa was the first to be accused of witchcraft in 1547. After years of an abusive marriage to conquistador Francisco de Ampuero, she admitted to

> "[THE HUNTS WERE] A RULING-CLASS CAMPAIGN AGAINST THE FEMALE PEASANT POPULATION. WITCHES REPRESENTED A POLITICAL, RELIGIOUS AND SEXUAL THREAT TO…THE CHURCHES… AS WELL AS THE STATE."
> *— Authors Barbara Ehrenreich and Deirdre English*

The Wizard of Oz introduced millions of Americans to the concept of a good witch in 1939.

with Indigenous midwifery were seen as the work of the devil."

Things were hardly better in the English colonies. On May 26, 1647, Alse Young of Windsor, Connecticut, was hanged at the Meeting House Square in Hartford, making her the first colonist executed for witchcraft. Historians suggest she may have been blamed for the influenza deaths of neighbors, or that the accusation was made when she tried to claim her inheritance following her husband's death (a woman asserting herself financially was a common way to find oneself named).

Forty-six other Connecticut residents would be accused and 11 executed before the state's final witch trial in 1697. Virginia never executed anyone, but tried 24 people, most notably Grace Sherwood, who was accused of killing crops and served eight years after not drowning in a swim test.

In the most famous American witch trials, more than 200 people were accused and 20 executed in Salem, Massachusetts, between 1692 and 1693. Although things quickly escalated, the first women named were once again societal outcasts who didn't like children, were on the outs with the church or dressed flamboyantly. By the 1700s, witch hysteria in much of the Western world had been officially outlawed, but the world remained leery.

THE TIME HAS COME

Over the past hundred years or so, the perception of the witch has again shifted. Beginning in the 1900s, independent ladies, on the advice of women's mags, began dressing as pretty witches at

visiting shamans in hopes of making her husband nicer. When that failed, she poisoned him with herbs. "The court didn't punish Sisa, who was protected by her class," says Pugh, "while the shaman was tortured to death."

According to historian Maria Emma Mannarelli's findings, during the second half of the 1600s, 184 people appeared before the Inquisition Tribunal in Lima, Peru. Of the 64 women, 49 were accused of witchcraft (only 11 men were). Once again midwives bore the brunt, says Pugh. "Any female healer was labeled a witch and punished, as rituals associated

Halloween parties—a huge courtship ritual of the day.

The world fully embraced the beautiful witch when Glinda floated down from her bubble in *The Wizard of Oz* in 1939. Oodles of likable witchy ones followed in pop culture, including nose-twitching Samantha Stephens in the 1960s sitcom *Bewitched*; the sexy sisters in *Practical Magic*; and *Harry Potter*'s ace student, Hermione Granger.

Pagan religions, with a focus on the phases of the moon and seasonal quarters, have been gaining widespread acceptance since the 1950s when Gerald Gardner and Doreen Valiente put Gardnerian Wicca on the map (for more, see page 53). And in the 1970s, Z. Budapest founded Dianic Witchcraft with women-only covens and a focus on the goddess. While "there is a certain amount of drama and flair to ritual magic," any sort of dark magic is frowned upon, Alex Mar, author of *Witches of America*, has said. The goal "is to bring yourself closer to spiritual enlightenment and balance."

Wicca was recognized as an official U.S. religion in the 1986 case *Dettmer v. Landon,* and is now one of the world's fastest-growing faiths. "Since the '80s, pagans have been gathering in outdoor festivals and…conferences all around the country," Mar told *Cosmopolitan*, adding that the internet opened the doors for those without a local community.

Witchcraft is more than a religion, though; the spiritual and the secular alike are drawn to the mythos. In the late 1960s, feminist groups like W.I.T.C.H. (Women's International Terrorist Conspiracy From Hell) began adopting the symbol of the witch as someone who bucks the system. And witches have become particularly active during the #MeToo and Black Lives Matter movements.

Even those sans cause have lately been experimenting with everything from candles to clothing inspired by the craft. Witches are now so popular *The New York Times* ran a story in 2019 titled, "When Did Everybody Become a Witch?"

"It's no surprise that in this time of great change, the witch is someone who resonates," says Grossman. "The witch is a symbol of rebellion, an outsider, someone long marginalized. She is about having power on her own terms."

Elizabeth Montgomery as the smart, sexy suburban housewitch Samantha Stephens changed the game on the sitcom *Bewitched*.

STILL HUNTED

IN SOME PARTS OF THE WORLD, ALLEGED WITCHES ARE ACTIVELY PURSUED.

While The Enlightenment brought the official end to witch hunts in much of the Western world, it was hardly the end of women (it's almost always women) being persecuted for perceived witchcraft.

Saudi Arabia is one of a handful of countries where it's still legal to execute witches. Its government even added an "Anti-Witchcraft Unit" in 2009 to "educate the public about the evils of sorcery, investigate alleged witches, neutralize their cursed paraphernalia and disarm their spells." That same year, two Indonesian women who'd been employed as domestic workers were convicted of witchcraft against their employers (one was said to have made a son disappear; he was found alive). They were sentenced to death, but were acquitted in April 2019, after 10 years in prison.

Witch hunts are technically illegal in India, but many rural parts of the country hold on to superstitions. Between 2000 and 2016, more than 2,500 Indian women were chased, tortured and killed, according to India's National Crime Records Bureau (experts think the true number is likely much higher). Often those witches or "dakan" are blamed for diseases and infant mortality, or sometimes they may simply have inherited valuable lands or property that an accuser is after.

Rachel shares scars from April 2017, when she was tortured with hot machetes after being accused of sorcery in her village in Papua New Guinea's highlands.

In some developing nations, hundreds of people—usually poor, older women, single mothers or the mentally ill—are killed annually in such countries as Kenya, Ghana, Tanzania, Papua New Guinea and the Central African Republic (CAR). "The accusation of witchcraft is a sentence without appeal," Nadia Carine Fornel Poutou, president of an association of female lawyers and advocates in CAR, told Al-Jazeera. "The Central African penal code is unable to establish what witchcraft is. Being a mystical matter, the authorities do not intervene."

Midwives, Wise Wives & *Witches*

The thin line between magic and science was often blurred in ancient and medieval times, with many healers accused of witchcraft and put to death for it.

During a time of grief, I began talking to the flowers growing in the field behind my farmhouse. I called these conversations "research." Each morning, I walked out to see which plant would catch my eye, then learned all of their names, stories and medicinal uses. Whenever possible, I sustainably harvested some for a salad, tincture or jelly. A great many of the plants I encountered had once been used to "provoke the menses," a common euphemism in past centuries for birth control. Some of these plants grew over the little spot in the field where my husband and I had buried our stillborn baby. Others came to me in the beautiful, weedy bouquets my young daughter liked to make.

These conversations with plants, I began to realize, were really a way of asking why we are born, why we die and what good we can do with the time in between. This research became more and more witchy all the time. My research was increasingly tied to the wheel of the year and rituals that honor the green world. I was especially obsessed with plants historically used for birth control— rue, Queen Anne's lace, pennyroyal, columbine—because so much of the

❋ Isis, the Egyptian goddess of magic, was also associated with marriage, fertility, motherhood and medicine.

❁ The ancient Egyptians believed magic was used to create the world, and celebrated goddesses like Isis (above, suckling her son Horus and right, offering a drink from a mystical tree to the deceased).

knowledge about those plants has been hidden or erased over the centuries. Some of the most efficacious plants ever used for birth control, like silphium, a member of the fennel family, have even become extinct. To better understand my beloved field and what her flowers had once been to women like me, I began reading the history of witch trials, which evolved into my essay collection, *The Witch of Eye*. Here is some of what I learned from working on that book.

MYTHICAL ORIGINS

Many of the so-called witches were first known in their communities as midwives, wise wives or cunning women. Today we would call them herbalists, botanists, ecologists or just doctors. The line between magic and science is thin. Why should some of us be struck down by a plague while others recover quickly? Why do some babies enter the world pink and squealing, while others fade into the gray mists of that other shore? To answer such questions, to martial the forces of health and vitality, to return a body to the fullness of life, requires deep learning and wisdom that might easily be interpreted as magic.

Some say the first spell was performed by the Egyptian mother goddess Isis, who was worshipped across the Roman Empire from around the fourth century B.C. until Christianity took hold in the fifth century A.D. The story goes that Isis invented magic to bring her husband Osiris back to life. According to myth, Osiris' brother Seth murdered him and chopped up the body; for a year, Isis roamed the Earth gathering up pieces. Then she molded the last bit she could not find out of clay. Was it his penis? His heart? His soul? Unclear, but with this last piece in hand, she breathed secret words that brought her beloved back to her. The magic only lasted a night, but that was long enough to conceive a child who would grow up to take vengeance on Seth.

Others say it was the ancient Greeks who invented both medicine and magic. Asclepius, the first doctor, was instructed in the art of medicine by the centaur Chiron. After his pregnant mother was killed by the god Apollo for infidelity, the newborn Asclepius was lifted from the ashes of her funeral pyre and given to Chiron for training. In "The Iliad," Asclepius staunches the wounds of soldiers on the battlefield with yarrow, much as midwives used the plant to stop a hemorrhage during childbirth Later, he

rendered some now-forgotten kindness to a snake, who licked his ears clean and then whispered secret knowledge into them. And so Asclepius became a magician-healer who could bring people back from beyond the brink. Although the knowledge of how to raise the dead died with him, Asclepius left behind his bag of magical healing herbs.

MAGIC GETS MALIGNED

By the 12th century, the associations between healing and magic were a source of suspicion. St. Hildegard of Bingen was a highly educated scholar whose writings on spiritual and physical healing were informed by her library of Middle Eastern medical texts and extensive experimental garden of medicinal plants. She was summoned to a tribunal of inquisitors to answer for herself, and it

✢ Asclepius, the Greek god of healing (above and right), is often shown with serpents that whispered their secrets to him.

Hausmännin confessed to killing 41 babies while working as a midwife. Her method of murder? She said her demon lover had given her a special salve she put in the expectant mothers' drinks, rubbed on the mothers' bellies or directly on the children. She also said she dug up the bones of children to make hail over the county. "She confessed likewise, that the blood she sucked from the child, she had to spit out again before the devil, as he had need of it to concoct a salve." She even confessed to using her ointment to bring about the deaths of several cows and a horse. The litany of her alleged crimes would be laughable if the circumstances hadn't been so deadly serious.

Under the pressure of their torture, Hausmännin took responsibility for every grief the village had ever suffered. If only she could have taken responsibility for all the comfort she'd given the village in her years as a licensed midwife—how many times she had delivered a baby, saved a mother, eased someone's pain or offered the choice and freedom of birth control.

was only her clever professions of faith (combined with her good luck to be born in a century before the bonfires began really blazing) that allowed her to escape unpunished. A great many of the women healers who followed her would not survive, and neither would the generations of knowledge they had inherited through oral traditions.

One such case was the widowed midwife Walpurga Hausmännin. According to court records from 1587, Hausmännin made arrangements to meet a male co-worker, Bis, for sex in Pfarrhof: "Him she enticed with lewd speeches and gestures." But at the agreed-upon hour, a demon named Federlin came to her in this man's clothes. After fornication, she felt the cloven hoof of the whoremonger, who promised to save her from poverty. She flew with him sometimes on a pitchfork. Those same records report that "the herein mentioned, malefic and miserable woman, Walpurga Hausmännin, now imprisoned and in chains has, upon kindly questioning and torture, following on persistent and fully justified accusations, confessed her witchcraft."

As a mystic, composer and theologian, Hildegard of Bingen was ultimately canonized (here and above) in 2012.

HERLINDIS

Hausmännin apologizes many times in these records. The judges seem to have convinced her she really deserved what happened to her. Centuries later, I want to absolve her of this cruel spell. After she was tortured and burned, her ashes were dumped in the nearest flowing stream. Having absorbed every crime, stillbirth, miscarriage, sick cow and misery the village had ever known, she was at least set free to wander with the water down through one forest and field after another.

BEARING THE BRUNT

Sadly, women healers were often the targets in witch hunts, not because they were practicing witchcraft, but because sometimes they knew how to save a life, which seemed miraculous, and sometimes they did not know what would help. Then, as now, healers simply could not give a satisfactory explanation for the mysteries of death, no matter how hard someone pressed them, so they became scapegoats for fear and grief.

Agnes Sampson, known as the Wise Wife of Keith, was respected in her community for the help she could offer—fertility treatments, assistance

> ### "[AGNES SAMPSON] HAD FOREKNOWLEDGE BY HER WITCHCRAFT OF DISEASED PERSONS IF THEY WOULD LIVE OR NOT, OR WHO WERE BEWITCHED PERSONS."
>
> ◆— *The trial of Agnes Sampson, Jan. 27, 1591*

and pain relief during labor, birth control and more. But that only lasted until 1590, when King James instituted extensive witch hunts in North Berwick, Scotland, to cope with the rumors, political intrigue and paranoia that plagued his court. By the time the king decided he wanted to interrogate this "wise wife" personally, she had been shaved bald and tortured with a rope around her neck for an hour after being pinned to a wall for days by the witches' bridle. Sampson began at last to confess after she was stripped naked and a suspicious mark that was said to be the place where the devil put his tongue was found on her privates.

Yes, Sampson admitted: She had given her patient, Euphemia Maclean, instructions for how to ease her labor pains. The medicine involved a powdered substance, a bored stone to keep under her pillow, and some "ichantit mwildis," which are the finger, toe and knee joints of a disinterred corpse. She also instructed Maclean to put her husband's shirt under the bed during her labor. For this so-called crime, which priestly men insisted was a sinful end run around God's punishment on all women for Eve's transgressions, both Maclean and Sampson were executed in 1591. (For more on Sampson, see page 46).

Another woman tried and executed was Lisbet Nypan of Norway. When questioned, she was only too glad to explain her methods for healing muscle aches and rheumatism. This had, after all, been her business for over 40 years. She would lay salts over the body of her patient and smooth them with massaging hands as she prayed. One

woman testified that Nypan cured her pains and agony by giving her a potion of soil, water and salt. She said this not with malice but gratitude…and confusion. Had Nypan sinned? Had she? How could this be wrong?

Nypan's husband was a prideful and short-tempered idiot. In disputes with neighbors he would raise his gnarled, 70-year-old finger and scold, "You forget who my wife is." I like him for the way he seems to have thought of himself as belonging to her as much as she belonged to him and for the way he was proud of her. He must have been very sorry, though, when he had to watch her die before they cut off his head.

During the trial, both Lisbet and her husband refused to confess to witchcraft or admit any wrongdoing. To Nypan, her inquisitors were nothing more than boys, part of a generation sent south to German seminaries to become an "educated" clergy, now returned home as young men obsessed with the spectral evidence and inquisition. She would never plead to such as these, and certainly she would never apologize for herself. Like generations of healers before her, she understood her practice to be a gift of wisdom and knowledge, one she'd been given by her god or gods to use well and share generously, but unfortunately she paid the ultimate price.

KATHRYN NUERNBERGER, *PhD, is a professor of creative writing at the University of Central Missouri. She is the author of multiple books of poetry and prose, including* The Witch of Eye, *a collection of essays exploring women who were accused and tried for witchcraft.*

Women Who *Resisted*

While tens of thousands of accused witches confessed in Europe and the Americas, some stood their ground.

Witch hunts became widespread after the Reformation of the church in 1517, when Protestantism began to spread throughout Europe.

✴ Those accused of witchcraft were often tortured into confessing demonic sexual acts and punished accordingly.

✤ Convicted witches were given brutal death sentences or tests to prove their innocence.

Modern witches call it "the burning times." Between 1300 and 1800, an estimated 80,000 people were executed for witchcraft in Europe and the New World. Thousands more were accused, with nearly all of them—around 80%—women.

There's no shortage of theories about what caused the witch hysteria. Leaders needed scapegoats for plagues and natural disasters; the Catholic and newly formed Protestant churches saw witch trials as a way to win new members; there was a clash between midwives (largely women) and doctors (mostly men). No matter the cause, many of the accused were brutally tortured— physically, mentally, sometimes sexually. Not surprisingly, these sleep-deprived, battered women often confessed, telling prosecutors exactly what they were demanding to hear—and of course, as part of their statement, they named other witches who'd conspired with them (this often came as quite a surprise to the unsuspecting newly named witch).

An accused person could often emerge from a witch trial alive, with only a small fine and public scolding, so long as she confessed contritely. Many of those accused would not have described themselves as witches prior to their trials—they only seemed demonic to witch-hunting members of the patriarchy because they were women who owned their own land, ran their own businesses or lived independent lives.

These women were tortured into confessions and their confessions then twisted into propaganda, with their stories told as cautionary tales to uphold an oppressive regime.

This was what happened in 1275 to Angela de la Barthe, an influential woman with property and wealth in Toulouse, France. Under the pain of torture, she confessed to giving birth to a wolf-headed, serpent-tailed child that fed on the fresh corpses of infants. Or so she might have confessed—there is some debate among historians about whether her trial happened at all, or whether her testimony was concocted 300 years after the fact in order to justify new witch hunts.

We do know that as a member of a gnostic sect of Cathars, de la Barthe would have believed in a dualist philosophy of a good god and an evil god who were equally powerful and held each other in balance. Toulouse was a stronghold of those who would resist the authority of the Church, and de la Barthe was among those who abandoned

> ### "WOMEN KNOW NO MODERATION IN GOODNESS OR VICE.... ALL WITCHCRAFT COMES FROM CARNAL LUST, WHICH IS IN WOMEN INSATIABLE."
> — Malleus Maleficarum, *1486*

baptisms, because she thought it absurd to buy holy water from a traveling priest when water is material and the spirit is immaterial. Like other Cathars, she would also have thought of the body as a mere vessel for the soul, making gender roles irrelevant distractions. But to inquisitors, a woman of independent means wielding authority was confusing and created a sense of bedevilment.

It was never the idea of a wolf-serpent son that bothered the witch hunters; it was the way she defied their rigid ideas about who was supposed to have power and who was not. This spirit of defiance and resistance can be seen in many of the women called to account for their power.

ROLE REVERSAL

The 1692–1693 witch trials in Salem were among the last, in no small part because Tituba, an enslaved woman in the village, completely upended their logic with her testimony. Unlike most of the accused, she never pointed the finger at anyone who had not already been named. When asked, Tituba said she could not make out any other names or faces and then collapsed to the floor as if entranced. Later, under further pressure, Tituba described nameless and faceless members of a coven. She noted how

✤ Being burned at the stake was a fairly common sentence for witchcraft in Europe.

King James I had a keen interest in witchcraft and was behind the persecution of hundreds of witches in the late 1500s.

they wore the fine clothes of well-to-do people, an ingenious detail that turned the wealthy elites of Salem, accustomed to scapegoating the marginalized and vulnerable, on each other.

Candy, another enslaved woman of Salem, also used her confession as an occasion to transform assumptions about who could be a witch and how. "Candy no witch, Barbados," she said, "In this country mistress give Candy witch." A judge asked Candy if she had signed the devil's book. She answered that her mistress had once shown her that her name was written in a book and she felt the presence of a great evil, the kind of thing the Puritans called "the devil." Candy reiterated, "Candy no witch in her country. Candy's mother no witch. Candy no witch, Barbados."

Margaret Hawkes, on the other hand, the white woman who imagined herself to own Candy, was a very real kind of monster profiting from a very real kind of pact with a devil. The records say that the afflicted Puritans in the room, upon hearing Candy's words and seeing her dunk some knotted rags in a bucket, "were greatly affrighted and fell into violent fits." Her testimony forced the upper classes of Salem to consider, for a moment at least, what you are when you say you have papers that prove you own someone else's soul. (For more on the Salem trials, see page 36.)

FIGHTING BACK

Isobel Gowdie was another whose trial was defined by her defiance. A professional storyteller in 17th-century Scotland, she was particularly admired for her flytes. Flyting is the art of flinging clever and well-crafted insults, common in oral literary traditions. Unfortunately, by the time her confession was recorded in 1662, she was long past the artful attention to puns that characterize a good flyte. Instead, she devoted her last public performance to asserting a violent and otherworldly power as she threatened, cursed and hexed the men in the room. You can almost see her spit the names of powerful people she says she pierced with fairy arrows as she flew through the sky like a straw in a whirlwind. It's worth noting that even these confessions employ literary techniques like assonance, alliteration and repetition. The Devil was 'beating and scurgeing'; bulls were 'crowtting and skrylling'; boys were 'whytting and dighting'." Even in her rage (perhaps especially in her rage) Gowdie was a poet.

According to historian Emma Wilby, Gowdie's trial for the witchcraft of insubordination was likely a consequence of wealthy landowners looking for theological justifications to maintain strongholds over the estates to which poor families like Gowdie's were tied as tenant farmers. Once, women had been allowed to flyte in the streets for the delight and amusement of their neighbors; suddenly, this became cursing, an illegal act of witchcraft. Once, you could gather with friends and family and complain about how the landlord just raised the rent again so how are you supposed to live. Now, you were a dangerous coven who wished to see him and all his heirs dead.

Gowdie seems like the kind of woman who knew she was alive by how

In the painting "Witch Hill/The Salem Martyr," a young girl is shown walking toward the gallows to be hanged.

fiercely she was fighting. She cursed Harry Forbes, one of her accusers, reciting three times the refrain: "He is lyeing in his bed and he is lyeing seik and sore, let him lye intill his bed, two monethis days more." Maybe she really was a witch; maybe she just really wanted to give certain men what she thought they deserved. Reading her words we can see, even centuries later, that so-familiar figure of the slumlord trying to distract from and forestall

his inevitable bankruptcy by crying witchcraft in the direction of anyone who grumbled at the sight of his face. We see an insolvent minister about to lose his congregation to rumors Gowdie repeated that he had an adulterous relationship with a servant. When Gowdie testifies, the trial cannot hold its glamour and we see how the judges were deranged with fear they might lose a kind of power they never should have had in the first place.

STANDING TALL

One of the charges levied against Maria Barbosa in 1610 was that she used her magic to invoke a sea devil. The specifics of her alleged spells are not itemized in the records of the witch trials in 16th- and 17th-century Brazil, but maybe she "destroyed many men" by putting water she had used to wash between her legs into her master's food, as a woman named Josepha confessed to doing. Or used a piece of cipó picão root for protection when she had to talk to her mistress, as Joanna had done. Perhaps she took scrapings from the soles of a master's shoes to prevent beatings, a spell allegedly used by enslaved people in Minas.

During these inquisitorial visitations, the official mission was to locate and punish those practicing Judaism in the Brazilian colonies, but trial records indicate judges were equally willing to police free African and Indigenous people to safeguard slavery and colonial rule. That was how an Afro-Brazilian practitioner of Indigenous medicine and spiritual traditions like Barbosa might find herself accused of witchcraft. On the way from Brazil to Lisbon to stand trial before central authorities, the ship was overrun by pirates. The men were all killed, she was taken as captive. Most likely she was raped repeatedly before being dumped on a beach in Gibraltar.

Picking herself up a world away from home, Barbosa decided to walk across this strange country into her own trial with her head held high. When she arrived, she asked for a cloak to cover her ragged nakedness after such a terrible journey. She asked this favor, she told the men in a clear voice, because she was not the woman they imagined her to be.

How remarkable is it that she still had the capacity to believe in another person's potential goodness—especially an inquisitor's? But Barbosa was among those women who used magic to give people some measure of control over their own lives. She wasn't asking those men for a cloak, she was offering them a chance to transform themselves. When they chose to ignore her dignity and be yet again as cruel, the way the moral authority shifted must have felt like the winds of some kind of judgment, perhaps a sea devil's, but perhaps that of a powerful divinity, passing through. —*Kathryn Nuernberger*

✻ A German woodcut from about 1550 shows two witches being burned at the stake, along with a beheaded "werewolf."

✻ Maria Barbosa was said to know many spells, including one that would invoke a sea devil.

33

1675

Sweden's Torsåker witch trials see 71 people executed in one day, most of whom were picked out by two young boys under the direction of Lutheran priest Laurentius Hornæus.

1645–1647

Following years of crop failures and devastating civil war in East Anglia, English villagers pay fanatical witch hunter Matthew Hopkins and his associate John Stearne to root out sorcerers. Using torture and dubious evaluations like the swim test and prick test, the pair are responsible for the execution of more than 300 witches—about 60% of the total number of accused witches executed in all of England.

1634

Father Urbain Grandier is accused of summoning evil spirits after Ursuline nuns claim they are possessed by demons in the Loudon, France, possession trials. Despite never confessing, even under torture, Grandier is burned at the stake.

1623–1631

During the Bamberg trials in Germany, nearly 1,000 people are accused and executed. Prince-Bishop of Bamberg Johann Georg Fuchs von Dornheim oversees the building of a special prison for the accused and confiscates their property. Torture is prominent in eliciting confessions. Eventually Holy Roman Emperor Ferdinand II is forced to issue a mandate against the persecution to stop executions.

1682

Following the scandalous Affair of the Poisons in the royal court (see page 48), King Louis XIV halts witch trials in France.

1675–1690

In the Salzburg, Austria, witch trials, 139 people are accused and executed. Most of them are members of a gang of homeless beggars led by Paul Jacob Koller—aka the Jackal—whose mother, under torture, said he had a pact with Satan. Unlike most of the trials, nearly all of the accused are male, and almost 100 of them are children or teenagers, with the youngest being just 10.

1691

Balthasar Bekker publishes *The Enchanted World*, the most famous book about spectral magic (it influenced Cotton Mather in the Massachusetts Bay Colony).

1486

Malleus Maleficarum is published and adopted by the church as a guide to witch hunts.

1500s

The Little Ice Age begins, causing decades of inclement weather and violent storms, resulting in crop failures. Witches are often blamed.

1517

The church splits into two factions—Catholic and Protestant. Now in competition, both use attention-grabbing witch trials as a way to lure members.

1532

Holy Roman Emperor Charles V declares witchcraft should be punished with death by fire.

1612

Ten people from the rural Pendle area of England are found guilty and executed at the Lancashire witch trials. More than half of the accused are from two feuding families, both of whom are thought to have advertised themselves as witches and healers.

1609–1614

The Spanish Inquisition investigates 7,000 people in Basque Country; 11 are executed or die from torture. To avoid punishment, so many come forward to confess, the judge becomes skeptical witchcraft is actually going on and dismisses pending cases.

1590

The North Berwick Trials start in Scotland with the confession of Gilly Duncan. Heavy torture is used to extract confessions. King James VI, who believes witches tried to kill him, personally questions Agnes Sampson. When he becomes King James I of England in 1603, he enacts harsh laws against witchcraft that require lower standards of proof.

1581

Johann Von Schönenberg is appointed archbishop of Trier, Germany, and sets out to purge his diocese of Jews, witches and Protestants. Between 1587 and 1593, 368 people are burned alive in the Trier Trials. Unlike many hunts, which focused on the poor, a third of the accused are nobility or hold positions in government.

1712

At the last official witch trial in England, Jane Wenham is accused of causing a girl to have fits. She pleads guilty, but a judge finds her innocent.

1736

In Britain, the Witchcraft Act is repealed, making it a crime to accuse someone of witchcraft.

1768

Under the rule of Empress Maria Theresa, Hungary ends witchcraft trials.

1782

Anna Göldi, a maid accused of sickening her employer's daughters, is tried and beheaded in Switzerland—the last known person executed for witchcraft in Europe.

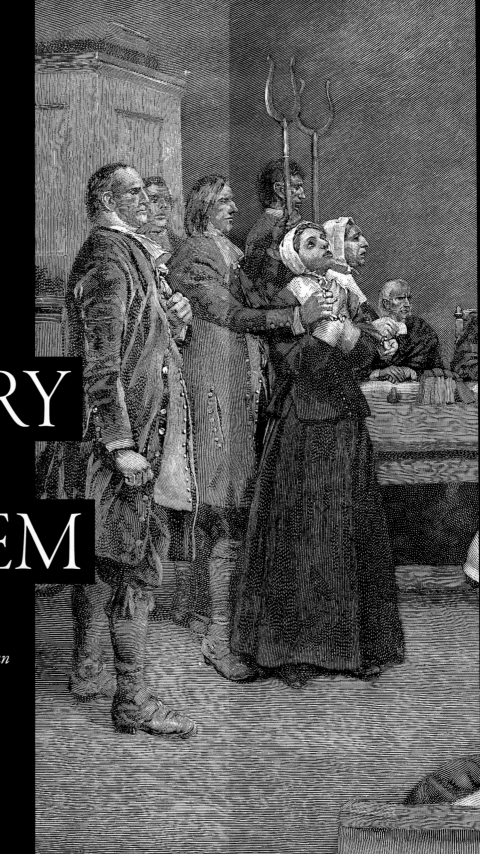

THE SAD STORY OF SALEM

No one was safe from the gallows when a frenzy gripped this sleepy Puritan town in Massachusetts.

Between February 1692 and May 1693, more than 200 people in Massachusetts were accused of witchcraft. Twenty were executed,

while others died in jail. And it all began with the odd behavior of two girls...

In 1692, Puritan Colonials were stressed over many uncertainties: how much self-rule England would allow; smallpox outbreaks; attacks on fisheries and trade; a war between England and France that led to frontier raids from French Canadian and Wabanaki forces. "None of this helped the economy and all of it aggravated local and personal conflict," says Marilynne K. Roach, author of *The Salem Witch Trials: A Day-by-Day Chronicle of a Community Under Siege*.

One such conflict involved Samuel Parris, who in 1689 had been ordained a minister in Salem Village—a rural part of Massachusetts some distance from the wealthier harbor area. "Three pastors had already come and gone," says Roach. "By 1692 a number of Village men stopped paying their share of Parris' salary." It was against this tense backdrop that Parris' daughter, Elizabeth, 9, and niece Abigail Williams, 11, began exhibiting strange behavior. They made bizarre sounds, threw things, screamed and clutched their heads.

Some scholars suggest the girls may have had epilepsy; others claim they were simply bored, imaginative children seeking attention. Another possibility: A study published in *Science* magazine speculated it may have been a result of "fungus ergot," found in grains common in the Colonial diet, which can cause similar symptoms and delusions.

No matter the cause, the families took the girls' "affliction" seriously. "A neighbor suggested an English folk remedy to the Parris' slaves John Indian and wife Tituba," explains Roach. "The use of the charm was to counteract supposed evil magic, but it seemed to frighten the girls more. They began seeing specters."

After home remedies and prayer failed, local doctor William Griggs posited the girls might be "under an evil hand."

THE HYSTERIA SPREADS

Within a week, the local law was involved. By this time, other Village girls—Ann Putnam Jr., Mercy Lewis and Elizabeth Hubbard—were also acting "as if invisible specters were after them," says Roach. The children claimed they were stabbed, choked and poked with pins by

✴ Bridget Bishop, hanged June 10, had been a pariah for dressing flamboyantly and having been married several times.

these ghostly apparitions, who took the shape of the person afflicting them.

On March 1, 1692, three Village outcasts were accused and arrested. Sarah Good was a poor beggar known to tease children. Sarah Osborn had been scorned for having an affair with an indentured servant. And Tituba, the Parris' enslaved worker from the West

Indies, was likely a pariah due to racism and her social status.

Local magistrates Jonathan Corwin and John Hathorne questioned the women for several days, reportedly looking for their "mark of the witch," and then sent them to jail where they would await trial. Osborn and Good maintained their innocence.

Tituba first denied any witchcraft, but finally said she herself had been harassed by witches, who forced her to pinch the girls. She spoke of cats, wolves and riding on sticks, and said Osborn owned a creature that had the head of a woman. In a later interview with Robert Calef for his book *More Wonders of the Invisible World*, Tituba said the

> **"LATER, ['CONFESSED' WITCHES] EXPLAINED THEY HADN'T KNOWN WHAT THEY SAID. BUT THESE APPARENT CONFESSIONS SEEMED TO PROVE A CONSPIRACY OF WITCHES REALLY WAS AFOOT."**
>
> *Author Marilynne K. Roach*

Rev. Parris had beaten her until she confessed, and then instructed her what to say when questioned, which may explain why her tale was so consistent with tropes of demonology. (After the trial, Parris refused to pay Tituba's jail fees and sold her).

"Her statement was taken to be a confession," says Roach. Tituba implicated Osborn and Good, and soon others were rounded up, questioned and held for trial. Among them: Dorothy Good, Sarah's 4-year-old daughter, whose "confession" was used against her mother; Martha Corey, who had questioned the credibility of the afflicted girls; Elizabeth Proctor, whose husband, John, was arrested for objecting during her questioning; and Rebecca Nurse, a 71-year-old woman so esteemed that more than 30 members of Salem Village wrote a letter defending her.

While the first arrests had been women disliked by the community, many of these newly accused were upstanding members of the church, making some uneasy. But nothing could get you accused faster than challenging the system.

By late May, a new royal governor, William Phips, arrived to find jails in three counties filled with suspects. Capital cases were usually tried in Boston, but Phips gave the green light to create a local court in Salem, where Lieut. Gov. William Stoughton would preside.

SUSPECT SPECTRALS

Bridget Bishop, an outcast for her lax church attendance and multiple husbands, was the first woman to face a jury in The Court of Oyer and Terminer. As with the others accused, she had no lawyer on her behalf, and most evidence was "spectral"—generally testimony of those who claimed she was attacking them via an apparition. In the courtroom, anytime Bishop would look at one of her accusers, the girl would be "struck down" and could only be "revived" by Bishop's touch, according to Puritan minister Cotton Mather's account in *Wonders of the Invisible World*. Bishop was found guilty and hanged June 10, 1692, on what became known as Gallows Hill.

"One of the judges resigned at this point and the court asked a council of Boston area ministers for advice," says Roach. "The ministers (including Mather) cautioned against relying on spectral evidence alone but said they trusted the judges' good sense." This proved tragic, as Stoughton believed the devil could never fake the ghostly appearance of an innocent person—meaning if someone claimed to have seen your specter, you allowed it.

The panic spread to neighboring Andover. Frightened by the convulsions of the supposedly afflicted girls and fatigued by relentless questions from the magistrates, many of the accused also "confessed," only to later recant. Another reason to falsely fess up was that it could buy you some time: Confessors were reserved as witnesses

MARTHA COREY AND HER PROSECUTORS

❊ Tituba was accused of telling the Parris girls enchanted tales about witchcraft.

✻ George Jacobs Sr. (bottom right) was convicted after being accused by his granddaughter.

against their fellow conspirators, with their own trials delayed.

On July 19, five more women were hanged, including Sarah Good and Rebecca Nurse, who had briefly been pardoned by Phips. A month later, five more "witches" were executed, including George Jacobs Sr. and John Proctor (wife Elizabeth was convicted, but not executed because she was pregnant). Giles Corey (Martha's husband) opted to "stand mute" and was "pressed" to death with stones to try to force him to enter a plea. Eight more were executed on Sept. 22, among them Martha Corey and Ann Pudeator, a wealthy widow and midwife in her 70s.

Executions likely would have continued, but in October, the Rev. Increase Mather, Cotton's father and the president of Harvard, denounced spectral evidence, saying, "It were better that 10 suspected witches should escape than one innocent person be condemned." And Phips, who had been in Maine, returned to find more chaos; even his own wife, Mary, had been accused. He halted the trials, "while the government rethought the matter, pending advice from London," says Roach.

By winter, that advice hadn't come and jails were still full. Living conditions were so bad, five people died, prompting Salem to establish a Superior Court to handle remaining cases. Many judges were the same, "but this time spectral reports were not allowed as evidence," says Roach. Most cases were dismissed; three people were convicted, but Phips pardoned them. The court considered Middlesex County cases in February and found no one guilty, cleared two Suffolk County cases in April and dismissed the remainder of the Essex County cases in May.

Following the trials, many of the accusers changed their names and moved; Ann Putnam later apologized. In 1711, the court issued a Reversal of Attainder, overturning most convictions, and Gov. Joseph Dudley authorized monetary compensation to families. Salem Village changed its name to Danvers to distance itself from the tragedy.

AMY L. HOGAN *delights in writing about celebrities, cannabis and witches for a variety of publications. She currently lives in New Jersey with her husband, their two daughters, three cats and a chicken.*

THE CRUCIBLE

Arthur Miller set his 1953 play *The Crucible* during the witch trials, which he used as an allegory for Sen. Joseph McCarthy's anti-Communist "witch hunts" at the time. Though the characters were taken from the actual Salem trials, Miller took liberties with the story, making Abigail Williams (who was 11) John Proctor's spurned lover who accuses John and his wife as a form of revenge. "The play is not history," Miller said. "However, I believe the reader will discover here the essential nature of one of the strangest and most awful chapters in human history."

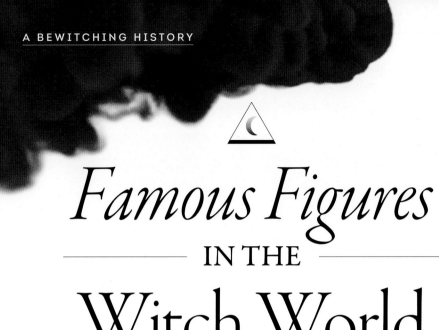

Famous Figures
IN THE
Witch World

Independent ladies, persecuted healers and modern activists—oh, my! Meet some of the craft's notable names.

✳ Eleanor Quinn's drawing of Kyteler, "An Irish Witch," appears in the book *Irish Witchcraft*.

DAME ALICE KYTELER
The Merry Widow

The witch trials in the 16th and 17th centuries dominate history, but Alice Kyteler of Kilkenny, Ireland, was accused of witchcraft in 1324, making her the OG of accursed European witches.

Born to wealthy Norman merchants in 1263, Kyteler was just a teen when she wed local banker William Outlawe. The groom died of a sudden illness a few years later, leaving Kyteler with a young son, William, and a healthier bank account.

Kyteler wed a second well-off moneylender, Adam de Blund of Cullen, shortly thereafter (the pair were briefly accused of killing her first husband but were never prosecuted), but the marital bliss was short-lived and de Blund died of a similar mystery sickness. Before his death, de Blund altered his will, leaving everything to Alice and William instead of to his own children. Kyteler said "I do" yet again to Richard de Valle, a wealthy Tipperary landowner, who later met a similar fate as his predecessors. Upon his death, Kyteler sued his son for her part of the inheritance.

Now one of the wealthiest women in Kilkenny, Alice also owned and ran her family's tavern, Kyteler's Inn, where she employed multiple beautiful women. The fine food, ale and, of course, the lovely ladies made it the most popular stop for locals and travelers alike. But some in town were less than pleased with Kyteler.

"The part which was beginning to upset her neighbors was that she was managing this herself, without the aid of a strong man," writes Anne Farrell in *Kilkenny Folk Tales*. "No matter how wealthy a woman became, she was always a target for the men who thought she was getting above herself." And novelist Niamh Boyce, who wrote a novel based on Kyteler, concurs that even more than her dead husbands, it was her business success that made Alice an outlier. "Kyteler was in fact a very powerful

❖ Irish artist Mick Minogue's "Alice" painting on St. Kiernan's Street.

❖ A life-size figure of Alice as the "merry widow" resides at Kyteler's Inn.

❖ Kyteler's Inn, established in 1324, is still a thriving pub with live music.

businesswoman, a very, very wealthy property owner and moneylender," Boyce told *The Journal*.

She got some side-eye in town, but the cauldron didn't bubble over until Kyteler married Sir John de Poer, who, you guessed it, began to fall ill a few years into the marriage. Reportedly his fingernails and hair fell out (consistent with arsenic poisoning). At first de Poer defended his wife, but he later changed his tune, saying he suspected he was being poisoned and had found a locked chest containing evidence of Alice's sorcery.

This did not go over well with his children, who found themselves disinherited after his death. Together with the children of Alice's other dead husbands, they brought complaints of *maleficium* (malicious magic) against their stepmother, claiming she had bewitched their fathers and killed them to benefit herself and her son. They took their grievances to Richard de Ledrede, the Bishop of Ossory, who had been eagerly awaiting any chance to defend his territory from heresy.

An investigation allegedly unveiled that Kyteler was the leader of a crew of demon-worshippers, mostly the women who worked for her. In addition to being husband murderers, Alice and her associates were accused of animal sacrifices and heresy. Kyteler was said to have gotten her powers from a lesser demon known as Robin Artisan, who appeared in various forms. Notably, Alice was also alleged to have had sexual relations with Robin—the first, though certainly not the last, time a woman was accused of doing the nasty with a nasty. (William Butler Yeats wrote about it in "Nineteen Hundred and Nineteen.")

Following torture, Kyteler's maid Petronella de Meath confessed to many of the crimes and implicated her employer. "Petronella said she had several times, at Alice's instigation and once in her presence, consulted demons and received answers," Ledrede wrote in his account.

Kyteler still had friends in high places—including her former brother-in-law, Chancellor of Ireland Roger Outlawe—who got a stay in the court proceedings, which allowed Kyteler to escape with Petronella's daughter. Neither was ever heard from again. Petronella was not so lucky, and became the first person burned at the stake for witchcraft. Kyteler's son William "recanted" and had to attend three masses a day for a year.

MOTHER SHIPTON
The Prophetess

Often compared to Nostradamus, Ursula Sontheil, aka Mother Shipton, is England's most famed prophet. Written in rhyming couplets, her visions are said to have foretold events including the Spanish Armada in 1588, the Great Plague of London that killed nearly 100,000 in 1665 and the city's Great Fire a year later.

But separating fact from fiction isn't an easy task. The first collection of Shipton's prophecies didn't appear until 80 years after her death, and Charles Hindley—who authored the most popular version in 1862—later admitted to making much of it up, according to an investigation by the British Museum.

Legend has it Sontheil was born to an unwed mother in a cave near the River Nidd in Yorkshire in 1488. With no family to help her out, her mother gave her, at around age 2, to a local woman, and tales of magical happenings—furniture moving on its own, dishes flying around the room—pepper her early years.

Reportedly hideously ugly, with a hunchback and crooked nose, Sontheil eventually returned to the area around her cave and taught herself to make natural remedies from flowers and herbs. At 24, she married carpenter Toby Shipton, and they set up home near Knaresborough. She continued her herbal practices and also began telling fortunes. Eventually her acclaim as a soothsayer drew people from far and wide, and she became known as "Mother Shipton."

Unlike so many other witches of the period, Mother Shipton wasn't prosecuted for witchcraft, but died of natural causes in 1561, an event she also is said to have predicted. Her cave and the adjacent petrifying well remain popular tourist attractions.

MOTHER SHIPTON'S CAVE

MOTHER SHIPTON STATUE IN KNARESBOROUGH

Shipton foretold of iron ships, aircraft and the execution of Mary, Queen of Scots.

King James leapt up and called Sampson a liar; she whispered a secret from his wedding night, convincing him of her dark powers.

Scotland" tell how Sampson maintained her innocence.

King James, who had recently married Anne of Denmark and felt that storms impeding their royal return had been brought on by witches, took a personal interest in Sampson's case and had her brought to the Palace of Holyroodhouse so he could question her himself. She refused to confess; the monarch didn't take it well. He had her shorn, stripped and tortured, looking on with "great delight." Sampson held out for days, before admitting to multiple crimes including causing a storm that drowned a noblewoman, conspiring with the devil and excavating bodies for spells. She was burned at the stake on Jan. 28, 1591.

But Sampson may have gotten the last laugh; her ghost reportedly haunts Holyrood Palace.

LOTTE VERBEEK AS GEILLIS DUNCAN IN *OUTLANDER*

AGNES SAMPSON
The King's Nemesis

Trained in the "black arts" by her father, Agnes Sampson was a prominent "cunning woman"—a healer who made occasional clairvoyant predictions—in the small village of Nether Keith in East Lothian, Scotland, according to *Witchcraft in Early Modern Scotland*. Her clients included commoners as well as low-level gentry, and earned her the nickname the "Wise Wife of Keith." Alas, her renown made Sampson an easy target when witch hysteria took hold of Scotland.

In 1590, Sampson was already in custody for suspected witchcraft when fellow accused witch Geillis Duncan (who inspired the *Outlander* character) named Sampson and several others in her confession, launching the North Berwick trial. This was the first Scottish witch trial under laws newly established by King James VI, a misogynist so obsessed with sorceresses he wrote his own guide to hunting them. Around 70 people were accused, and most confessed under torture, but reports in the "Newes From

ISOBEL GOWDIE
The Tell-All

Isobel Gowdie may just be the biggest oversharer in the history of the craft. Thousands of women and men were tortured into giving confessions during Scotland's witch trials, but over six weeks beginning on April 13,1662, in the village of Auldearn, Gowdie, an illiterate farm wife, offered up four intensely detailed confessions unprompted by torture (though modern scholars suggest she was likely still mistreated and sleep-deprived).

In her confessions, published in Robert Pitcairn's 1833 *Ancient Criminal Trials in Scotland,* Gowdie claims to be a member of a coven in the service of Satan and she doesn't hold back on the details of her carnal relationship with the devil. She admits to multiple acts of *maleficium,* including destroying her neighbor's crops, using a child's body stolen from the grave, and burning effigies to cause death and suffering to local leaders and their offspring. She claims to have turned herself into various animals and to have participated in witches' Sabbats, and named 12 other women (her confession is what historian Margaret Murray used as the basis for her theory that covens have 13 members). She also offered extensive talk of her dealings with fairies in her testimony—dining with the fairy king and queen, who was "brawly clothed in white linens."

Scholars have posited Gowdie may have been suffering from psychosis (although others suggest she was a gifted story teller; see p. 31 for more). Though no one knows what happened to her after the trial—there is no record of her execution—Gowdie continues to inspire. She's been a character in many novels and TV shows, and Scottish composer James MacMillan even wrote a symphony about her, "The Confession of Isobel Gowdie."

❋ Ian Howard shows the lady and her demon in his mixed media "Isobel Gowdie Portrait."

LA VOISIN
The Craft in the Court

Behind the gilded gates of Versailles, France, some poisonous practices were afoot, and smack in the middle was famed sorcerer Catherine Monvoisin, aka La Voisin.

Born in 1640, La Voisin had "visions" all her life, but only got into fortune telling after her husband's jewelry business went belly-up. La Voisin also worked as a midwife and performed illegal abortions, reportedly burning and burying thousands of fetal remains in her garden.

According to Anne Somerset's *The Affair of the Poisons: Murder, Infanticide, and Satanism at the Court of Louis XIV*, La Voisin began to see a pattern to her clients' desires; almost everyone who came to have a reading wanted a lover or an inheritance. So the enterprising clairvoyant, who often performed in a custom-made red velvet robe embroidered with gold eagles, cashed in on her clients' desires, and started selling amulets, love potions, poisons and rituals. She even began brokering "black masses," where clients could pray to Satan for a wish to be granted.

By the 1660s, La Voisin had achieved considerable fame and fortune with a client roster including a good chunk of French aristocracy, such as Duchess of Bouillon Marie Anne Mancini and Duke of Luxembourg François-Henri de Montmorency. She lived in Villeneuve-sur-Gravois, and had lavish parties with the Parisian aristocracy in her garden.

In 1667, noblewoman Madame de Montespan allegedly hired La Voisin to hold a black mass, where she prayed to win the love of King Louis XIV. "I saw my mother bring in an infant... obviously premature and place it in a basin over which [the priest Étienne] Guibourg slit its throat, draining the blood into the chalice...speaking the names of Madame de Montespan and the king," La Voisin's daughter Marguerite testified, according to *Sex With Kings: 500 Years of Adultery, Power, Rivalry, and Revenge*.

Apparently it worked; de Montespan became Louis' official royal mistress and bore him seven children. Whenever a problem arose in their relationship, de Montespan would seek help from La Voisin, who set up multiple masses and furnished her with love potions.

When Louis took a romantic interest in Angelique de Fontanges in 1679, an enraged de Montespan allegedly asked La Voisin to kill both the king and his new lover. After initially protesting, La Voisin put an unsuccessful plan in motion to murder the king with a poisoned petition. Angelique did die, and while an autopsy found natural causes, a household servant named Françoise Filastre admitted under torture that she had poisoned her on behalf of de Montespan (though she recanted before her execution). La Voisin, her daughter and other acquaintances were arrested. Unlike many others accused of witchcraft, La Voisin was never tortured, although an order had been issued to allow for it.

Scholars speculate that with her extensive ties to the court, a confession might have proved devastating to the upper class. Though she never confessed to helping de Montespan, La Voisin did admit: "Paris is full of this kind of thing and there is an infinite number of people engaged in this evil trade."

Put to trial and convicted, La Voisin was burned at the stake. After her death, her daughter told of de Montespan's murderous plans. Embarrassed by the ordeal, Louis terminated the investigation and de Montespan continued to live at the court for the next decade.

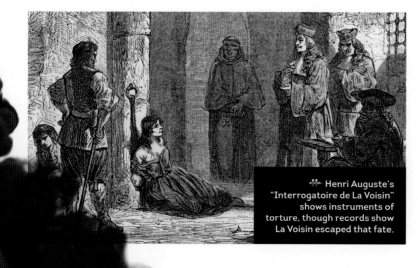

❧ Henri Auguste's "Interrogatoire de La Voisin" shows instruments of torture, though records show La Voisin escaped that fate.

LE PORTRAIT DE LA VOISIN.

Source de   tant de maux maudite creature
Qui par mille poisons destruisoit la Nature,
Si la parque en fillant tes detestable jours
A fait regner la Mort, en prolongeant leur cours,

PAINTING OF
MARIE LAVEAU

MARIE LAVEAU
The Voodoo Queen

New Orleans is a city known for its otherworldly occurrences and occupants, but none is as famed as Voodoo Queen Marie Laveau. Nearly 150 years after her death, tourists still flock to her tomb in St. Louis Cemetery No. 1, and follow the ritual of drawing three crosses while asking Laveau for a favor.

A free woman of color, Laveau was born in the French Quarter in 1801 and was raised primarily by her grandmother—a formerly enslaved person—who taught her in both the traditions of Catholicism and Voodoo. At just 18, Laveau married Haitian immigrant Jacque Paris, but less than a year later, her groom mysteriously disappeared, and she began calling herself the "Widow Paris."

Shortly after, Laveau began a relationship with French nobleman Christophe Dominick Duminy de Glapion. Because he was a white man,

✳ Laveau's tomb was the second-most visited grave in the U.S. (after Elvis Presley's Graceland), but in 2015, officials limited visits to guided tours.

the two were not allowed to marry, but they lived together until his death in 1855, and reportedly had seven children (one of whom herself became a Voodoo practitioner, Marie Laveau II).

A healer and herbalist, Laveau also worked as a hairdresser. Her clients included some of the city's most prominent women, as well as their servants. Everyone knows people tend to get chatty while sitting in the stylist's chair, and historians have speculated

✤ Angela Bassett looks fierce as Laveau in *AHS: Coven*, but the show took liberties with Laveau's history.

that Laveau's celebrated clairvoyant abilities may actually have been that she pieced together secrets from her vast network of clients. Either way, she always seemed to have just the thing to fix any situation.

Voodoo had negative connotations at the time, but Laveau, who remained a devout Catholic, combined elements from both faiths to reach a wider audience. She famously led public Voodoo rituals full of dancing and singing in Congo Square and, despite strict segregation laws, people of all races came to participate.

Some feared Laveau and spoke of terrible things happening to those who crossed her. Local newspaper *The Crescent* called her "the notorious hag who reigns over the ignorant and superstitious as the queen of the voodoos." But she was also widely revered for her powers, and people traveled great distances for her counsel. She reportedly dispensed charms and potions to heal the sick, and she even saved condemned men from the gallows.

Upon her death of natural causes in 1881, *The New York Times* ran a lengthy obituary, claiming: "Besides knowing the secret healing qualities of the various herbs...[Laveau] was endowed with more than the usual share of common sense, and her advice was oft times really valuable and her penetrations remarkable. Adding to the qualities the gift of great beauty, no wonder she possessed a large influence in her youth and attracted the attention of Louisiana's greatest and most distinguished visitors.... Lawyers, legislators, planters, merchants all came to pay their respects to her."

Laveau continues to enchant us today, and has served as the inspiration for dozens of books, films and songs, including a Marvel Comics hero (see image at left) as well as Angela Bassett's character in *American Horror Story*.

✳ "You get peace, and contentment and joy," Gardner said of being a witch.

Gardner blesses Wiccan witch Patricia Dawson and magician Arthur Crowther at their wedding in 1960.

GERALD GARDNER
Wicca's Founding Father

Known by the craft name Scire, Gerald Gardner was hugely influential in bringing contemporary Wicca to the mainstream. (For more on Wicca, see page 70.)

Born to wealthy parents from the United Kingdom on June 13, 1884 (which was a Friday, of course), Gardner was a sickly child and spent much of his youth in warmer climates, including the Canary Islands and Ceylon (now Sri Lanka), where he developed his lifelong curiosity about Indigenous cultures and weaponry. As a young man, he worked as a tea and rubber farmer in Ceylon, Borneo and Malaya, and he continued studying local customs and religions as well as Freemasonry.

It was in the late 1930s that Gardner discovered practicing pagans, and became initiated in the New Forest Coven, a group he believed were descendants of a pre-Christian witch cult. "I then knew that which I had thought burnt out hundreds of years ago still survived," he said.

From then on, Gardner actively promoted his beliefs. "He wasn't a religious pioneer," writes biographer Philip Heselton. "What he did was publicize it and write about it, and he gradually became known through that.... He initiated quite a lot of people into the Wiccan culture. He felt it was important that it survived."

Though Gardner kept many of the coven's rituals secret, he did extensively detail their 1940 "Operation Cone of Power." In the midst of World War II, the New Forest Coven erected a "Great Circle" with a form of magical energy known as a cone of power that they sent to Berlin, hoping to prevent Nazi forces from crossing the English Channel and entering England. The effort was so exhausting, he said, several members died shortly after.

Gardner wrote multiple books on the craft, including *A Goddess Arrives*, *High Magic's Aid* and 1954's *Witchcraft Today*, which led to an epidemic of scandalous headlines lamenting black magic was alive and well in England.

When the U.K. repealed laws against witchcraft in the 1950s, Gardner struck out on his own and became the "resident witch" at Cecil Williamson's Museum of Magic and Witchcraft. He brought Doreen Valiente into his coven, and she helped him rewrite and expand his *Book of Shadows*, putting more emphasis on worshiping the goddess. This text remains one of the most influential in contemporary Gardnerian Wicca.

Since Gardner's death from a heart attack in 1964 while aboard a ship off the North African coast, critics have found fault in some of his work, claiming he borrowed heavily from others like Aleister Crowley, that he encouraged coven members to stretch the truth about their lineage, and that he placed more emphasis on men and less on the goddess. But his influence on contemporary witchcraft still looms large. "Of course I'm a witch," Gardner once said. "And I get great fun out of it."

ROSALEEN NORTON
The Witch of King's Cross

Born in 1917 in New Zealand, Rosaleen Norton spoke of having visions as a child and even recorded the appearance of her "witches mark" on her knee at age 7. This didn't go over particularly well in school, where she was expelled for drawing demons and vampires. After dabbling with service jobs and writing horror stories for publications like *Smith's Weekly*, she studied art at East Sydney Technical College in Australia.

In her early 20s she began reading about different types of esoteric mysteries, including the Kabbalah and the work of Aleister Crowley. These led her to the practices of trance and sex magic.

Among the community of artists and poets in the bohemian area of King's Cross in Sydney, Norton became widely known for her art, her pansexuality and her coven. Norton would describe her work as "psychic experiments" and said she used drugs to help access her unconscious mind. In addition to selling her work, she also made money through the sale of charms and hexes.

She exhibited a series of sexually explicit drawings with pagan themes at the University of Melbourne in August 1949. Police raided the exhibit and she was charged with obscenity. While her art was widely admired and critically acclaimed, almost every exhibition or publication was attacked under obscenity laws. She was also prosecuted when photos of her private sexual rituals became public. Still, Norton stood for what she believed in. She passed away in 1979 from colon cancer.

❊ "Norton's esoteric beliefs, cosmology and visionary art are all closely intertwined," wrote biographer Nevill Drury.

SYBIL LEEK
The Prolific Priestess

Sybil Leek, once dubbed "Britain's most famous witch," was born in 1917 and grew up in Hampshire. She learned about astrology and divination from her Russian grandmother and herb lore and Eastern philosophy from her father. Leek claimed she was descended from the 18th-century witch Molly Leigh and that her family's connection with Celtic witchcraft could be traced back much further.

In her teens, Leek was initiated into a French coven located in the hills above Nice. On her return she joined the renowned Horsa Coven (which reputedly existed for over 800 years), becoming its High Priestess.

During the 1950s, while walking in the woods, Leek had a vision that her life's work would be to promote the Old Religion. Her reputation as a witch and psychic spread and brought tourists to the village where she lived. She was a striking figure, often wearing a cape and a large crystal necklace, and walking around with her pet jackdaw on her shoulder.

✤ Leek (here in 1963 and at left in 1964) declared herself to be "just an ordinary witch from the New Forest in England."

Constant press attention and a hostile attitude toward her as a witch led to her emigrating to the U.S. in the early 1960s. Her book *Diary of a Witch* was published in 1968 and she quickly became popular on the media circuit. She worked primarily as an astrologer and wrote nationally syndicated newspaper columns. For many, she was their first exposure to the craft, and they liked what she said.

"[People] are searching for a religion where they don't have to live a godlike life, a religion that acknowledges them as human beings," she told reporters.

She published more than 60 books on witchcraft and the occult over her lifetime. Until her death from cancer in 1982, Leek continued to promote an understanding of the craft, although her beliefs, particularly an opposition to drugs and nudity in rituals, would often see her in conflict with other witches. Today, a coven of white witches still meets in the New Forest following her teachings.

✳ "Witches use witchcraft as a science, an art and a religion," Cabot has said.

LAURIE CABOT
Salem's Keeper

Modern witches owe a debt of gratitude to Laurie Cabot, who has spent decades dispelling misconceptions about the craft.

Born Mercedes Elizabeth Kiersey in 1933, Cabot always had an interest in witchcraft and claims she was often in trouble as a child for sharing info she picked up through extrasensory perception (ESP). When she was a teenager, her family moved from California to Boston, where she began exploring witchcraft at the public library. At 16, she participated in a ritual, where she vowed: "I return to Earth my wisdom and I call myself witch."

Following her second divorce in the 1960s, Cabot decided to take that vow to the next level and live "totally as a witch." She began wearing dark robes and black eye makeup. "Putting on the black gives me peace of mind and a magical surge," she has shared. "Black absorbs light, giving me strength and more psychic power, so that I may do more magic and more healing." She adopted the name Cabot, claiming she is from a long line of witches from the Boston Brahmin Cabot family.

Committed to educating others, she authored several books on witchcraft and opened new age shops, which garnered national attention when one was featured on *Bewitched*. Upset by negative portrayals of witches in pop culture, she founded the Cabot Tradition of the Science of Witchcraft and the Witches' League for Public Awareness. "Our religion has no evil deities; our philosophy requires no fear tactics to function, only education and enlightenment," she wrote.

For her advocacy, Cabot was named "The Official Witch of Salem" in 1977 by Massachusetts Gov. Michael Dukakis.

SANDRA RAMOS
*The Purple Lady
in the Woods*

As a teenager in the 1960s, Sandra Ramos rebelled against her conservative upbringing by running away from home and dating older men. "I thought those things gave me power," she reflects.

But when she discovered Z. Budapest's brand of feminist Dianic Wicca and met activists like Florence Kennedy, she realized there could be even better ways to rebel against the establishment. "I consider myself a witch," says Ramos. "A witch is a woman who is in touch with her power. She is someone who knows we have a strength the patriarchy can't take away."

Taking the goddess spirit to heart, the New Jersey resident oversaw the creation of multiple shelters for women and children who were victims of domestic violence. Currently her Strengthen Our Sisters organization (strengthenoursisters.org) offers multiple services to those in need, including child care, education and legal aid. And at 79, she says she has "so much more to do."

But for the young residents in Ringwood, New Jersey, Ramos is known for being the joyful witch who hugs trees, sings, drums and has a penchant for purple...a big one. Her house (in the woods, naturally) is purple; so is her car, her clothing, even her hair. "Children love it," she says. "They relate to magic."

❊ Sandra Ramos has always marched to the beat of her own drum—and she's happy to bring it to rallies for women's rights.

❊ Often asked when she'll grow up, Ramos says, "I hope never!"

CHAPTER 2

WITCHES TODAY

LEARN ABOUT THE ROOTS OF MODERN WICCA AND WHAT REALLY GOES ON IN A CONTEMPORARY COVEN. DISCOVER HOW SORCERESSES HAVE BECOME FEMINIST SYMBOLS, GET THE LOWDOWN ON WITCHY WARDROBES, AND HOP ON YOUR BROOMSTICK TO HEAD TO SOME CRAFTY DESTINATIONS.

Getting *Witchy*

The craft's intersection of feminism, environmentalism and self-care is a huge draw for many people seeking something outside of traditional religions.

❧ Online retailers report crystals and other mystic objects have soared in popularity in recent years.

With December 21 rapidly approaching, Jennifer James was busy building an altar to usher in the pagan holiday of Yule in her San Diego living room. Her ornate chalice, mini cauldron, silver pentacle, vibrant scarlet and evergreen candles, and new incense were all primed and ready to go for Winter Solstice prayers, thanks to purchases on Etsy and The Witches Box, a $75 monthly subscription service offering a curated collection of sacred objects and texts.

"They not only send you the candles and oils and incense, but they send you exactly what to say for the ritual—that's cool, because I don't really know what I'm doing yet," admits James. An aspiring author and licensed family therapist, she has only recently begun practicing Wicca after connecting with two like-minded friends she met through the woman-focused empowerment network known as Warrior Goddesses. Although they reside in different time zones, the three middle-aged confidantes now meet on Zoom Thursday evenings to check in and conduct spells for abundance and healing that call on the "Divine Feminine."

"I was looking for something that was more pro-woman, more empowerment and I really feel like this is it. Goddesses and nature-based spirituality and Wicca: If you are going to look for a feminist religion, this is it," says James.

❧ With magical supplies just a few clicks away, witches like Jennifer James can easily set up a home altar.

> **"[WICCA] MAKES ME FEEL LIKE I CAN MOVE IN THE WORLD IN A DIFFERENT WAY THEN I MOVED IN THE WORLD WHEN...FOLLOWING CHRISTIANITY OR EVEN BUDDHISM."**
>
> *— Jennifer James*

DRAWN IN

What resonated about Wicca for James and her friends is what also drew other early practitioners to nature and female-centric worship in the late 1960s, when paganism and its subsect of witches first emerged out of the shadows in the United States. It was the dawn of first-wave feminism and the sexual revolution, along with a rise in environmental consciousness. Now, in the digital age, with climate change, gender and racial equity top of mind, neo-pagan spirituality once again captures the zeitgeist of the unsettling times that saw both the rise of Trumpism and the alt-right but also ignited powerful social movements pushing back on

the white establishment—notably Black Lives Matter and the Women's Marches. Historically, witches have been demonized and forced to worship underground, but they also have a legacy of fighting for the disenfranchised and bucking the dominant culture.

"As a child, I remember questioning everything. Why are they telling us these stories and why do we have to believe them? I've always been a seeker of what else is out there," shares Phoenix-based yoga therapist Lara Rosenberg, a friend in James' Goddess cohort who was raised in a traditional Jewish home.

Today, seekers like Rosenberg and James have to look no further than their iPhones for information,

not to mention connection to vibrant communities 24/7.

"There is a public awareness now that I think is much greater than it has ever been in the past," says Sarah M. Pike, PhD, chair of the comparative religion department at California State University, Chico, and a modern paganism researcher who has been studying the witchcraft movement since the mid-1990s. Although high-tech and nature-worship may seem at odds, Pike says many witches and neo-pagan practitioners worked in the computer industry in its earliest days and found each other through nascent internet message boards and blogs. E-commerce and social media gave them an even bigger platform to emerge from the proverbial broom closet and to connect with each other online and at pagan festivals. The explosive growth of Facebook, Twitter and the like has ignited even more curiosity and, for better or worse, the commercialization of sacred practices. "Normalization can be a mixed bag for pagans," says Pike of the potential risks for the faith to be oversimplified or trivialized now that it's in the spotlight once again.

Google queries for tarot cards, crystals, sorcery and shamanism have been on the rise since the search engine began tracking data in 2004. Fueled in part by a growing consumer interest in wellness, the online marketplace Etsy reports a surge in searches for mystical items. The hashtag "witch" has millions and millions of posts on Instagram ranging from galleries of dreamy witch-inspired artwork to directions for using talismans and glossy ads for courses and healing products. The Warrior Goddesses group through which James and Rosenberg met has nearly 300,000 followers on its IG account (@warrior_goddess_training).

JUNIOR WITCHES

But it's perhaps #WitchTok, a subchannel of the teen-dominated platform TikTok, that may be the most quantifiable indicator of how witchcraft has suddenly permeated pop culture once again. The hashtag WitchTok had garnered 11 billion views by March 2021,

featuring bite-size videos of "baby witches" with hundreds of thousands of followers hawking "spell jars," demonstrating how to cast hexes and throwing shade at critics who dismiss their magic as fun and games.

"We are having a second wave of teenage witches, thanks to the TikTok witches," says Helen A. Berger, PhD, a Brandeis University sociologist who says the first wave of teen witches in America occurred in the 1990s when a flurry of

A DISCOVERY OF WITCHES

books and TV shows like *Charmed*, *Buffy the Vampire Slayer* and *Sabrina the Teenage Witch* inspired teenage girls and some boys to explore the world of Wicca. Hollywood is tapping into the trend again with TV shows dramatizing witchy storylines, including *Chilling Adventures of Sabrina*, *A Discovery of Witches* and *Motherland: Fort Salem*.

"When something becomes popular, whether it's high-top sneakers or witches, it takes on a life of its own. Even if you weren't interested, you think, 'I should take a look,'" Berger says.

HERE TO STAY?

While witchcraft is having a moment online, it's not entirely clear if this translates into more people identifying as religious followers or whether they're just dabbling. Pike explains there is a wide spectrum under the pagan umbrella, from those who observe rules and specific deities to people like James,

⁂ Shows like Netflix's *Chilling Adventures of Sabrina* helped prompt a renewed interest in witchcraft, especially among young women.

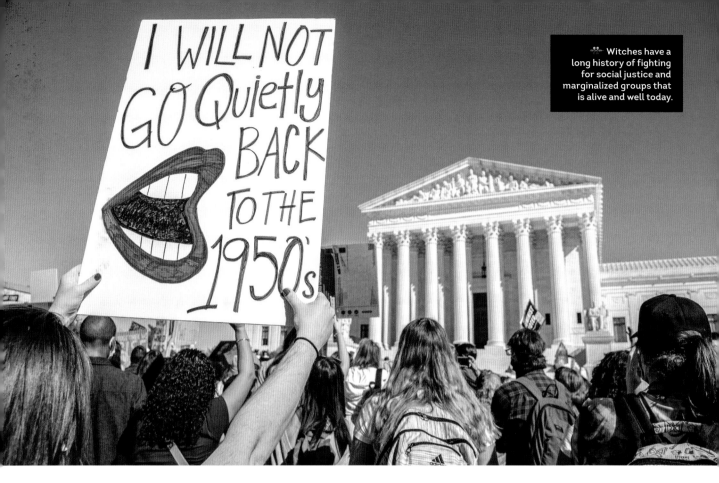

who is experimenting with her witchcraft practice and creating as she goes.

That's also why it's hard to quantify just how many witches there are in the U.S. A 2014 Pew Research Center study put the number at 0.4% of Americans, or between 1 million and 1.5 million people, who identified as Wiccans or pagans. Berger's most recent research, published in her 2019 book, *Solitary Pagans: Contemporary Witches, Wiccans, and Others Who Practice Alone*, reported that more than three-quarters of those she surveyed practice their faith alone or as "solitaries," meaning they're not affiliated with a formal group or leader.

In many ways, it's precisely that autonomy that prompted James to study Wicca when she became disillusioned with Christianity. She was raised by a Methodist pastor in a conservative home in Ventura, California, and by age 18 found herself trapped in an abusive marriage. She shudders as she recalls her ex-husband reciting passages from the Bible about women submitting to their husbands when she tried to fight back. He later left her, and she would go on to train as a family therapist working at a domestic violence clinic where she met other women who shared similar stories of feeling betrayed by their own Western faiths. After practicing Buddhism, James has found peace and a spiritual home with her fellow Goddesses. "I am more of a powerful force to be reckoned with

now then when I ever was following an Abrahamic religion or even Eastern philosophy, because they are more male-centered," she says.

As her altar preparations continued at home, this new witch focused her prayers to the Goddess for a better year ahead. "A psychic told me that in the coming year 'I will rise like cream.'" James says. "So I will be wishing that all the things come my way including getting a literary agent, publishing my book, getting a promotion at work and maybe finding a partner."

HEATHER CABOT *is a New York-based speaker, journalist and author of* The New Chardonnay: The Unlikely Story of How Marijuana Went Mainstream.

"Some of the biggest myths are people asking if I can fly or why my skin isn't green," says hereditary witch Bambi. "Don't get me wrong, I enjoy *The Wizard of Oz*—just not people's assumptions that witches are supposed to look like the Wicked Witch."

Dispelling *Myths*

Practicing witches talk about some of the biggest misconceptions they encounter about the craft.

If you've watched a movie or read a book in the past century, you might think that witches fly around on brooms and sacrifice babies to stay young and beautiful. Pass one on the street and she might curse you, just for kicks. Or maybe you believe witches are mysterious and powerful, but you have to be born into a long line of healers to explore magic. At the very least you'll have to change your religion, right? These self-identified witches are here to set the wand straight.

MYTH WITCHES WORSHIP THE DEVIL

"The most common misconception is that witchcraft is some fashion of devil worship. That couldn't be further from the truth. First and foremost, not everyone believes in the devil. In this context, 'the devil' is almost always synonymous with the Christian archetype, which is precisely that, an archetype of one faith. Secondly, anyone who has ever made a birthday wish while blowing out a candle has performed magic. Realistically, witchcraft is just prayer with flair—we light incense, candles, sometimes we have crystals spread out, and otherwise project a prayer out into the universe."
—*Temperance, a spiritual consultant and tarot reader, who writes about life and everyday witchcraft (thepeacockwitch.com)*

"Witches work with nature and the moon cycles; some of us don't even believe in the devil. People think we're out to harm others; we're not."
—*Meleny Rose Villaman, an ancestral witch and tarot reader*

"People have all these ideas that witches dance around a circle at midnight waiting for the devil to bring you doughnuts and bagels. If you want that, you'll have to bring your own.

"There's a big difference between being a Satanist and being a witch. I grew up in a very Christian community—all fire and brimstone—where people would often say, 'Oh the devil made me do it.' Your partner was abusive, your grandson robbed a bank—the devil made them do it. That takes away free will. Being a witch is very much the opposite; it's about making your own choices. You do it, you own it. You can't just blame things on the devil when you're a witch."
—*Rhonda Harris-Choudhry, a spiritual counselor, "very public witch" and author of* You Are Not Broken *(healinghennagoddess.com)*

"There are centuries of bad and false history because of the Burning Times (the witch hunts in Europe; for more, see page 26) and earlier that went on for 200 years. Women were rounded up, tortured, burned and drowned because of their knowledge of healing and magic. Women have been feared for our connection to the Goddess since before 1600 B.C. This is changing now, because many people are feeling a pull toward their ancestral origins and a longing to explore goddess mystery."
—*Melissa Waite Stamps, a priestess of the Goddess, energy worker and feng shui designer (melissawaitestamps.com)*

MYTH ALL WITCHES ARE WICCAN

"'Wiccan' and 'Witch' are not the same. Wicca is a religious practice under the pagan umbrella. I'm an eclectic practitioner; I'm more spiritual than religious, though I do have deity elements in my practice. But not all witches practice Wicca."
—*Temperance*

"Wiccans are witches, but not all witches are Wiccan. Witches also don't care about who is a certified high priestess or priest, and who took this course or that course. Our ancestors were witches without all these shiny certificates. Certificates don't make someone a real witch. You can absolutely be a witch and maintain your other identity or religion. I know witches of many backgrounds and beliefs. I've come across witches who are also Christian, Catholic and other religions. Witches who are atheist or pagan, witches who believe in karma and don't. We are all our own witch."
—*Bambi, a hereditary witch, herbalist and certified energy healer (the-lotus-moon.com)*

MYTH MAGIC IS EVIL

"Witches have been accused of eating babies, causing hexes that destroy people's lives, causing crops to die and famine. It's actually the opposite. Priestesses, witches and all women of goddess lineage are healers, midwives, psychopomps, who accompanied the dying through their death experience. They were able to connect with ancestors and spirits to bring through knowledge of other dimensions: the phases of the moon, stars and sacred Earth."
—*Melissa Waite Stamps*

"I might get in trouble for saying this, but when people talk about Jesus performing miracles, it sounds like magic—turning water into wine, feeding a whole community with one fish. It's certainly not being used for evil. People of his time believed in magic, and it plays into his message. Use your magic to do good."
—*Rhonda Harris-Choudhry*

"I don't appreciate that witches are still sprinkled with dark connotations in TV and film. Everything on this planet is pure energy. We're all made up of vibrating molecules; witches have simply decided to interact with that energy on purpose and with intention. We go through our days making conscious decisions to notice nature, to notice patterns and the small things that so many people look past."
—*Temperance*

"Walking past a witch or looking at one does not mean you have been cursed. That takes a lot of time and energy and more than likely we won't waste that time and energy on anyone. "
—*Bambi*

"I am a Wiccan and I believe in the Wiccan Rede. That means what you put out into the world comes back to you times three. So that's a pretty big deterrent to hurting people."
—*Meleny Rose Villaman*

MYTH WITCHES WEAR ALL BLACK

"I'm not very fashionable. I like those long, thin sweater things. No shoes most of the time. Rings, bracelets, crystals stuffed in multiple places, pockets, bra, you name it. I'm so not a stylish witch; I go for comfort."
—*Bambi*

"One of the most dangerous misconceptions is that you'll be able to identify someone as a witch based on her looks. As far as clothing, witches are connected to nature, so clothes that are made of natural fabrics are prized: linen, cotton, wool and silk. Jewelry

☙ "Some people believe witches are evil and need blood as sacrifice," says priestess Melissa Waite Stamps. "This is not true."

"Satan doesn't really even exist in witchcraft unless you belong to a faith that believes in a concept of the devil," says author Rhonda Harris-Choudhry.

made from natural stones and metals is also valued."
—*Milana Perepyolkina, a healer and author of* Gypsy Energy Secrets: Turning a Bad Day into a Good Day No Matter What Life Throws at You *(gypsyenergysecrets.com)*

MYTH I DON'T KNOW ANY WITCHES

"As far as I'm concerned, everyone practices witchcraft. If you've ever put on a nice dress and some perfume when you're going out hoping to meet someone, you're casting a spell. Or if you're making your famous soup for a loved one when they're sick—the intention is to heal; in a way it's a potion. One of the most prominent examples can be seen in sports: Cheerleaders dance and chant to rile up the energy of the crowd. They get the audience to chant with them, filling their energy with the intention that their team will win. Most people are already practicing magic; they just don't realize it."
—*Rhonda Harris-Choudhry*

"Think about making a cake: While stirring the batter, you think good thoughts for the people you want to share it with. Want to spice up your morning brew? Take a spoon and sir in some extra clarity and focus. These small everyday witchcraft practices are things many people do without thinking about them. People have just been conditioned to believe it's some nefarious thing.

"I like to make things: crochet, sewing, painting, baking…. These are all physical representations of the essential process of magic. Plus, handmade crafts can be filled with so much love, you can literally imbue that feeling into the thread as you're putting it together. The act of crafting…taps into the exact same intuitive outlet that guides our magic."
—*Temperance*

67

THE REAL WITCHES

THERE'S NOT A CHILD-EATER AMONG THESE CRAFTY WOMEN!

TEMPERANCE

MILANA PEREPYOLKINA

MELENY ROSE VILLAMAN

RHONDA HARRIS-CHOUDHRY

BAMBI

MELISSA WAITE STAMPS

MYTH BECOMING A WITCH IS COMPLICATED

"There's absolutely room on the broom for newcomers. Find someone you feel drawn to and learn from them. Read, read, read! But, at the same time, don't believe everything you come across. Unfortunately, there are some people throwing out information that's harmful."
—*Bambi*

"The advice I gave my daughter is: If you want to be a witch, all you have to do is decide that you're a witch. It's that easy.

"Nowadays, I'm seeing people getting their toes wet after discovering a tarot deck or some other divination tool. And that's actually perfect! There is no 'right' and 'wrong' when it comes to magic. Be wary of anyone who tells you that you're 'doing it wrong.' Do what you feel called to do, but do be aware of why you're doing what you're doing. No two people walk the same path, and it's OK for your practice to look different from the next person's—tap into your inner voice because that's where the magic is."
—*Temperance*

"You start life with intuition but you lose touch with it as you get older. Find ways that help you reconnect.

"Everyone learns in different ways. You can look for meetings and groups in your area—there are a trillion groups on Facebook. Not everything is going to be for every person, so find traditions and practices you connect with. If you love plants, earth magic might be for you. If you want to heal people look into water magic. If you want to find deities for guidance, look into those traditions.

Exploring takes time, but find where your passions lie." (For more, see page 130.)
—*Rhonda Harris-Choudhry*

"[You] might want to join a goddess circle, or group that explores Wicca or other pagan path. Spend time in nature, look at your passions in art, culture and history, and find a corresponding lineage of Magic, Goddess Mystery and paganism.

"Follow your intuition. There are so many amazing resources out there. If you get involved with a group or pick up books that talk about demons, black magic, using your magic to hurt or control others—run. You want a pure hit without negative propaganda. Find resources

that support the pure original impulse for where all of this amazing knowledge began. It's a beautiful adventure."
—*Melissa Waite Stamps*

"Get in touch with the Earth. Being a witch means I am deeply connected to the Earth, the sun, the moon and the stars and to all the elements—the air, water, fire, wood, metal and ether. It means every moment of my day is sacred and connects to the spirits around me. It means things around me are alive and interacting with them brings me joy and wonder. It means I fill every minute of my life with meaning and gratitude!"
—*Milana Perepyolkina*

❧ Despite what Hansel and Gretel would have you believe, "We do not eat children!" says Bambi.

The World of *Wicca*

A look at how the pagan faith became one of the fastest-growing religions in America.

The goddess has been looking for her children.

"She comes in dreams and speaks to their hearts," explains New York City–based attorney and bestselling author Phyllis Curott about Wicca's female deity. "Other women and men go seeking her. They know something is missing. They long for meaning deeper than our celebrity-dominated culture. There is a hunger for contact with something that gives a true sense of purpose."

Curott says people of all ages and races are finding those answers in the study and practice of Wicca…and she would know; she's a Wiccan priestess.

The first thing to understand about contemporary Wicca is that it has nothing to do with bubbling cauldrons, satanic worship and summoning demons. Consider it more of a revival of pre-Christian traditions that embrace and honor the goddess and her consort, a god, as well as the changes of the seasons and the moon phases.

The ritual practices of Wicca include things like casting spells for healing and protection. And rituals often invoke the five classical elements—air, fire, water, earth and ether (spirit). Those elements are represented in the five points of the pentagram, the most frequently

GARDNER'S *BOOK OF SHADOWS*

used symbol of Wicca. Ironically, the pentagram is one of the things that led to the religion's bad rap. It's actually the reverse pentagram, where two points face upward, that has been associated with summoning evil. But as Mary Matunis, MTh, explains, to some, Wicca "[appears to] dance close to the satanic side with the magic and the pentagram, because it's got such a bad association already."

But most Wiccan holidays are exuberant celebrations embracing the totality of life. Aging, death and sickness are included, but the nature of the practice is joyful. And many of those, such as New Year's and May Day, are things already celebrated in other religions that were simply rebranded. "Wicca provides tools for people to have really profound experiences," Curott says. "You're given techniques so you can go on a spiritual journey and discover the world is in fact divine and sacred."

✤ The Witches' Cottage was a coven meeting place in Bricket Wood, England.

✤ Many people consider British author Gerald Gardner the father of modern Wicca.

HISTORY LESSON

Pagan traditions go back thousands of years, but Gerald Gardner is generally credited with putting modern Wicca on the map. Inspired by practices and beliefs of a group of witches in southern England, he was initiated into their New Forest Coven in 1939. Gardner created a master list of beliefs, principles, spells and rituals, which he called *The Book of Shadows*. In the late 1940s, he began utilizing it as a guide for those he inducted into his own Bricket Wood Coven (many covens and individual practitioners still create their own Book of Shadows today). After England repealed laws against witchcraft in 1951, Gardner created the modern Gardnerian Wicca movement. In 1954, he released *Witchcraft Today*, which was the first mainstream appearance of "Wica" (the extra "c" was added in the 1960s). The book was met with some sensationalized headlines and pearl-clutching, but ultimately the nature-based rituals he details helped usher in a resurgence of the worship of the mother goddess and her male counterpart, the horned god.

Gardner died in 1964, but throughout the '60s and '70s, Gardnerian Wicca spread from the U.K. across other English-speaking countries and divided into multiple "traditions" including Georgian Wicca, the female-centric Dianic Wicca, and Eclectic Wicca, which encompasses traditions from different sects. While there are variations among sects, most follow some version of the Wiccan Rede, created by Gardner's protégée, priestess Doreen Valiente, in the early 1960s. It can be best summed up as, "Do what you will so long as it harms none."

Leek and her jackdaw perform a ritual dance in the New Forest in 1964.

"MAGIC CHANGES YOU.... WICCA CAN SHIFT OUR PERCEPTIONS AND OPEN UP OUR CONSCIOUSNESS SO THAT WE ARE ABLE TO SEE AN EXPANDED REALITY, WHICH IS ABSOLUTELY REAL."

— Wiccan priestess Phyllis Curott

British businessman Raymond Buckland is believed to have brought Wicca to the U.S. in 1962. Four years later, he opened the museum of witchcraft on Long Island, New York, and by 1973, he had founded a new branch called Seax-Wica, largely inspired by Anglo-Saxon paganism. But it was another British expat, eccentric antiques dealer Sybil Leek, who made Wicca a household name in the U.S. "I am a white witch and I come from a line of white witches, who exist only to do good," she told London's *Daily Express*. Leek introduced her version, called "Celtic Witchcraft," to the West Coast when she left for sunny Los Angeles.

Leek made a name for herself in Hollywood as the author of a dozen books, including *Diary of a Witch* and *The Complete Art of Witchcraft*. In 1964, she memorably appeared on an episode of the daytime game show *To Tell the Truth*, where she delighted and spooked the celebrity panel with her spellbinding story. "We are a much larger organization than the Mafia, only we don't hold board meetings," she quipped about Wiccans.

Leek died in 1982, but would no doubt be proud the U.S. government officially recognized Wicca as a religion in 1985. Since then, membership has boomed. A study conducted by the Pew Research Center in conjunction with Trinity College found there are potentially 1.5 million practicing witches in the U.S. alone—that's more members than the Presbyterian Church.

A WITCH'S PLACE

What's causing this awakening of witches? "It's a spiritual practice that really suits the modern temperament," explains Curott, noting that people today tend to be skeptical and more educated than in the past. "Wicca is appealing because nobody is asking you to give up your rationality…. You are not required to believe in a god you have never seen, or dogma. It's not a mechanical approach to the supernatural; it is a divine approach to the natural. The discovery that you have the means of effectuating change in yourself as well as the world around you is empowering and uplifting."

That can be especially appealing to women or gender-nonconforming people who may have felt constrained by conservative religions. "That happens when someone becomes disillusioned by more traditional faiths," says Matunis. "Wicca is more freeing and the female Mother Earth power is attractive."

Pennsylvania mom Holly M. credits Wicca with drastically improving her outlook. "My life is calmer. I get answers quicker when I have a decision to make," she shares. "Some of my techniques are just going outside and listening. Being pagan is very peaceful. It also teaches you how to build healthy boundaries with people; you recognize who is being toxic."

An added benefit of Wicca is it doesn't require treks to church, and an altar can be fashioned nearly anywhere. "I was born into Wicca and have always been spiritual," shares Joanne B. "I knew I had magic since I was a child. I honed my premonitions and gifts quietly."

Curott concurs: "There is something to be gained in isolation. In nature you need to be silent, fully present and focus on what you hear, smell and see as well as what's whispered in your ear and what you hear in your heart." But finding a coven can be even more magical, especially when others can teach their practices.

Sandi Liss, who runs SoulJourney Bookstore in Butler, New Jersey, agrees. "The benefit of working together is raising the energy. Multiple hands make for better, lighter work. And it brings about a sense of community and inclusion."

No matter how you practice, Curott says, Wicca allows you to "take off the blindfold that's been tied on by history, by habit, by culture and to see the sacred in the world around you." —*Amy L. Hogan*

KNOW YOUR NEW AGE TERMINOLOGY

DRUIDISM is a modern movement that celebrates a harmonious connection with the natural world. Most early Druids identified as Christian.

HEATHENRY models its practices on the pre-Christian beliefs of the early Middle Ages. They honor their deities and spirits with a ceremonial toast of alcoholic beverages.

NEW AGE refers to the religious and spiritual beliefs that boomed in Europe and America in the 1970s.

OCCULTISM isn't a religion but the study of the occult, which is secretive practices. Non-Jewish forms of Kabbalah are considered occult.

PAGANISM is the umbrella term for any religion, especially those that emphasize nature, that isn't one of the world's main religions.

SATANISM sprang up with the Church of Satan in 1966 and has two main groups: theistic Satanism, which views Satan as a patriarch, and atheistic Satanism, which uses Satan as a symbol of human traits.

WICCA is a nature-oriented religion whose rituals and practices are derived from pre-Christian beliefs.

WITCHCRAFT, as a religious practice, involves magic and is usually associated with an affinity for nature.

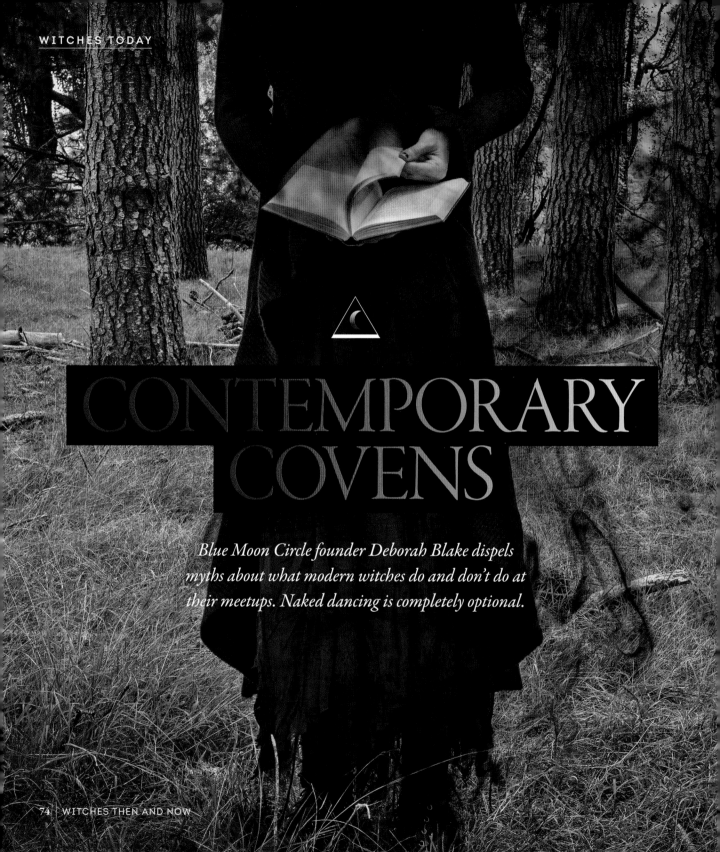

CONTEMPORARY COVENS

Blue Moon Circle founder Deborah Blake dispels myths about what modern witches do and don't do at their meetups. Naked dancing is completely optional.

IF SOMEONE SAID THE WORDS "WITCHES' COVEN" TO YOU, I SUSPECT IT WOULD CONJURE UP IMAGES THAT ARE DARK AND CREEPY, AND POSSIBLY A BIT SCARY.

Or at the very least, it's something far removed from everyday life. Thirteen women, dancing naked around a bonfire beneath a full moon chanting strange and esoteric words while casting evil spells on their enemies. Possibly with black cats.

While a fascinating concept, that image really only exists in stories. The modern coven bears little resemblance to the stereotypes so many people believe. There might be dancing, a bonfire and a moon, but that's about the only realistic part— and even those are optional.

Consider this your guide to the *real* witches' coven, parting the curtains of superstition and misinformation to show you the world of the modern witch.

To begin with, let's dispel a few myths. That whole "evil" thing, for instance. The wicked witch is a fictional creation, originating in fairy tales and books like *The Wonderful Wizard of Oz*. In real life, a witch is generally someone who follows a nature-based religion, usually worships both a god and a goddess, and

believes that magic is real and can be used to create positive change. (This is a simplistic description, since there are many different kinds of witches, and not all of them would describe themselves this way. But for the sake of this article, these are the folks I am talking about.)

Witches usually believe in some variation on "the law of returns," which says that what you put out into the world comes back to you. Many call it the "threefold law" and say things come back times three. If you put a curse on someone, it is just as likely to rebound on you. Kind of cuts down on the evil, if what you do is going to come back and bite you on the broomstick! Many witches also believe in the importance of free will, which precludes casting any spell that would influence another. The one exception to this is defensive magic.

More than that, though, witches are, for the most part, just regular people who follow a different spiritual or religious path. They are your neighbors

and sometimes your friends or relatives. They're no more likely to be evil than anyone else. Are there bad witches? Of course. There are also bad Christians, Jews and Muslims, but none of these folks are representative of the group as a whole.

Another myth: Witches are all women. There are male witches, too. Witchcraft in general is a very open and accepting practice, and therefore tends to attract those who may not feel welcome in other religions, so there are many LGBTQ witches as well. A coven may be made up of all women (mine is), or a mix of genders.

Nor does a coven have to be made up of 13 members. This number is traditional, but these days, groups can be either much smaller or much larger. Some community covens number in the hundreds. My own group, Blue Moon Circle, has had anywhere from three to 11 members over the years.

❧ "Our magical work encompasses everything from healing to prosperity to working on growth, balance or focus," says author Blake of her coven.

As for the naked dancing...well, that is purely a matter of choice. There are some groups who practice "skyclad" (naked), but participants in most covens are more likely to wear cool witchy garb like black robes or amulets, or simply the same clothes they wear the rest of the time.

WHAT REALLY HAPPENS

So let's talk about which parts of our image are actually realistic. Covens *do* gather in a group, no matter the size. The occasion is often when there's a full moon, which is considered to be a powerful and sacred night, dedicated to the goddess.

We also often get together for the eight Sabbats, or pagan holidays, which fall on the solstices, the equinoxes and four cross-quarter days in between. You might be surprised to know just how many Christian and secular holidays are derived from these pagan celebrations. Christmas, for instance, shares many traditions with Yule, the winter solstice.

We do often sing or chant, drum, dance or use other music or movement, mostly to raise energy, but also just as a form of celebration or to honor the gods. If the weather and surroundings allow, there might be a bonfire, but it isn't necessary. While most coven gatherings include some form of spell work, the Sabbats are likely to include a feast made up of foods suitable for the season, like my favorite corn casserole at the midsummer harvest festival Mabon, or homemade bread at Lammas, which celebrates the start of fall.

BLUE MOON CIRCLE

The modern witches' coven I know best of course is my own. In 2004, after spending five years in a coven led by my first high priestess and completing a year and a day of instruction by her to prepare me for leading my own coven, I started a group called Blue Moon Circle.

In the beginning, there were only three of us: me, Jhaea and Morghana (I'm using their witchy names to protect their privacy). I came from a relatively traditional coven, whereas the other two had both spent many years as solitaries—witches who practice on their own—because they had never been able to find a group that fit them. In the beginning, we were strangers. Today we are best friends, even family.

Although my training was mostly Wiccan-leaning, the other two tend to take a more general approach. These days, we usually call ourselves "eclectic witches," which means we use a little bit of whatever works. This is fairly typical of modern covens, where members often come from different backgrounds.

We currently have four regulars, and usually meet for the Sabbats, sometimes with friends who have been coming on and off for years. When we can, we also get together for full moons. And we almost always have a feast after the ritual!

Because we live in upstate New York, we can only use the permanent outside circle during the nicer weather, and the rest of the time we meet in my living room. And no...we don't dance naked, but we have been known to drum and chant.

A COVEN OF YOUR OWN

If you're interested in joining a coven, finding a group on your own can be daunting. Depending on where you live, there may be many, or none, and they may be hidden from outsiders.

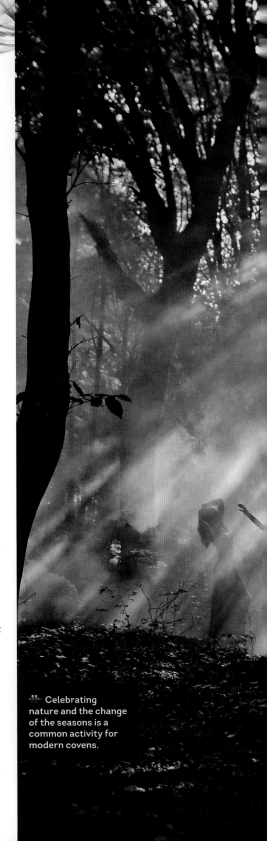

Celebrating nature and the change of the seasons is a common activity for modern covens.

"MOST BOOKS ON WITCHCRAFT WILL TELL YOU THAT WITCHES WORK NAKED. THIS IS BECAUSE MOST BOOKS ON WITCHCRAFT WERE WRITTEN BY MEN."

✦— *American Gods and* M Is for Magic *author Neil Gaiman, on how many modern misconceptions about covens got started*

If you know other witches, don't be afraid to ask around. Check message boards at places like a new age shop or a health food store. Some Unitarian Universalist churches have pagan members and host groups. Of course, you can also search online.

Keep in mind that all covens are not the same. Look for one that best suits your needs and personality. If you're easygoing, you're not going to want a strictly observant group, for instance. Ask how the coven is run, what the expectations are and how open it is. And if something feels off to you, listen to your gut.

If you can't find an existing coven that suits you, you can always do as I did and start your own with like-minded friends or agreeable strangers. It's important to make sure everyone is clear about what they are looking for in a group and that you all have the same basic goals and approach to witchcraft. If there are folks who aren't "out of the broom closet," be sure everyone who attends is willing to respect the privacy of those who are members. As with any other relationship, open communication is the key to success—that, and a little bit of magic.

DEBORAH BLAKE *is the author of multiple paranormal novels and nonfiction books about the craft, including* Modern Witchcraft *and* Everyday Witch Oracle.

From *Curse* to Rallying Cry

Modern feminists have reclaimed what it means to be called a witch.

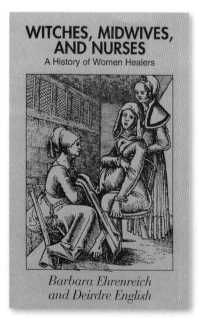

WITCHES, MIDWIVES, AND NURSES
A History of Women Healers

Barbara Ehrenreich and Deirdre English

Go to a rally for any progressive cause and you're likely to see shirts and signs with messages like "Radical Feminist Witch" or "We are the daughters of the witches you couldn't burn." There might even be women (and men) wearing full-on witch costumes.

"Witchcraft and feminism go hand in hand," says Kirsten Bazet, a longtime witch who's spent a decade studying pagan traditions in New Orleans. "Witches have been oppressed throughout time, and now they are breaking the chain and reclaiming the title—not of someone who creates evil, but someone who creates change and betterment. If that doesn't scream feminism, I'm not sure what does."

A HISTORY OF BUCKING THE SYSTEM

With Jennifer Aniston making headlines for holding a "goddess circle" on her 50th birthday and Lorde telling reporters she's "basically a witch," it might seem like this connection between the witch and the feminist is a newish thing. (And there's certainly been a barrage of retailers peddling everything from sage candles to spell books as witchy feminist chic.) But women's rights and the craft go waaaaayyyy back.

"For thousands of years, a witch has been a healer. She has been the strongest member in her community, a wise woman people turned to when in trouble," says Milana Perepyolkina,

"MORE AND MORE, WOMEN ARE BOLDLY CALLING THEMSELVES WITCHES. A WITCH IS ALWAYS INDEPENDENT, AND WHEN A WOMAN CALLS HERSELF A WITCH SHE OWNS HER POWER AND IS PROUD OF IT.

Author Milana Perepyolkina

❋ Ros Baxandall of the feminist activist group W.I.T.C.H. casts a Halloween Hex on Wall Street on Oct. 31, 1968.

> **"THROUGHOUT HISTORY, STRONG WOMEN HAVE BEEN CALLED 'WITCH' SO THEY CAN BE PUSHED INTO A CORNER OR PERSECUTED. IT COULD MEAN ANYONE WHO DID NOT CONFORM TO SOCIETAL STANDARDS."**
>
> ✦ *Author Préity Üpala*

author of *Gypsy Energy Secrets: Turning a Bad Day Into a Good Day No Matter What Life Throws at You*. "That power frightened men in the past, and it is frightening men even now."

Indeed, many of the women accused of witchcraft during the Western world's witch craze from the 1200s to the 1700s were actually midwives and cunning women, whose knowledge of homeopathic remedies posed a threat to male-dominated fields like science and medicine. Plus, with herbal methods of birth control and abortion, they offered women a chance to control their own fertility—and thus their own lives. It's a phenomenon Barbara Ehrenreich and Deirdre English chronicled in their 1973 book *Witches, Midwives, and Nurses*. (They rereleased the text in 2010, as it was—sadly—still seen as being relevant.)

Other women accused were often those who didn't follow religious or cultural practices of the time. Among the evidence presented against Bridget Bishop, the first woman executed in Salem, Massachusetts, in 1692, was that she dressed flamboyantly, was known to frequent taverns and had been married three times. Suffragist and abolitionist Matilda Joslyn Gage wrote about this back in her 1893 book, *Woman, Church, and State.*

These same characteristics of independence can be found in fiction, as well, from Circe turning men into pigs in "The Odyssey" to the young woman in *The Witch* who makes a deal with the devil to live deliciously. "Witches in literature have an air of independence and freedom; they seem to be living a life on their own terms, not conforming to society's expectations," says Préity Úpala, author of *New Feminism* and host of The Préity Effect podcast. "They were rebels and heretics. They seem to be having an adventurous, eventful life without being bogged down with household chores like raising children or taking care of a husband."

With these women and characters living as feminists before the term even existed, it only makes sense witches would have links to the modern movement, according to Carol Queen, PhD, author and cofounder of the Center for Sex & Culture (carolqueen.com).

"The history of witchcraft and neo-paganism from the latter 19th century to the 1950s included threads that involved sexual freedom and freedom from restrictive gender roles—mostly in a bohemian context—plus, there was an increasing interest in goddess worship," says Queen, who wrote her thesis on feminist Wicca. "People, and especially women, felt spiritual but were looking for something that wasn't sex-negative or patriarchal."

By 1968, an organization of socialist feminists went so far as to name

themselves W.I.T.C.H.—Women's International Terrorist Conspiracy From Hell. According to its manifesto: "W.I.T.C.H. is…an awareness that witches and gypsies were the original guerrillas and resistance fighters against oppression…. Witches have always been women who dared to be: groovy, courageous, aggressive, intelligent, nonconformist, explorative, curious, independent, sexually liberated, revolutionary. (This possibly explains why 9 million of them have been burned.)" Notably in the late '60s, they donned traditional witch garb and marched on Wall Street to put a hex on the male-dominated financial system, and also protested a bridal fair being held at Madison Square Garden.

By the time Queen got involved in feminist witchcraft in the 1970s, she says, "A cheeky radical feminist vibe was fully

meshed with another alternative culture emblematic of the 1960s—the ecological and sustainability movement. It included a spiritual reverence for the Earth and all living things. In some circles it also had the kind of interest in crystal healing and zodiac that is au courant today in many women's circles."

While Queen says this community has been thriving for quite some time in places like Northern California, the reemergence really kicked up with feminists in the '70s and '80s. "These were the building blocks that increasingly led second-wave feminists to witchcraft."

Flash-forward to 2016. The election of Donald Trump brought a compelling push to reclaim the word after Hillary Clinton—the first woman ever to be nominated for president of the United States on a major party ticket—was

Witches have made their case at protests supporting Black Lives Matter.

called a "nasty woman" and a "witch" by countless naysayers.

Many feminists just went with it. During his presidency and beyond, Trump was hexed by many a social media witch, as were #MeToo villains like Harvey Weinstein and Supreme Court Justice Brett Kavanaugh.

Lindy West made the connection explicit in publishing her 2017 *New York Times* editorial about calling out harassers, titled, "I'm a Witch and I'm Hunting You!" And that same year, Jess Zimmerman and Jaya Saxena boldly proclaimed in their self-help book *Basic Witches*, "If you speak when you're told to be quiet, take pride when you're told to feel shame…you're practicing witchcraft."

WHAT'S IN A NAME?

While the term might have some cool new cachet, a lot still depends on who is throwing around the word "witch" and in what context. A woman referring to friends as her coven can be a show of sisterhood, but having someone spit it out in anger, not so much.

"It can still be used very pejoratively," says self-described witch Maria Ramos-Chertok, author of *The Butterfly Series: 52 Weeks of Inquiries for Transformation*. "If a man is calling a woman a witch, it carries a dimension of male privilege. There's a whole history of patriarchal abuses that go along with that."

Ramos-Chertok also notes that while "witch" isn't necessarily synonymous with "bitch," the words have similar connotations. And she suspects some people might get a "perverse thrill" out of using the more acceptable witch.

Üpala adds even if the word is meant as one of endearment, it might still be offensive. "Some people might be sensitive to it, given the bloody history where you had women literally being burned at the stake." It's worth noting that in some parts of the world, the term not only carries negative connotations but potentially deadly ones. Witchcraft is still a capital crime in countries like Saudi Arabia, and thousands of suspected witches are killed annually by vigilantes in parts of sub-Saharan Africa.

Even if you're not going to be persecuted for using the word, it's important to consider that for longtime members of the community, the term is more than a T-shirt. "Some people are only obsessed with the pop culture," says Bazet. "Magic and witchcraft aren't toys or selling gambits; they should be treated with respect. It takes a lot of study and understanding to practice."

Queen agrees the new masses of Instagram and TikTok witches can occasionally be frustrating. "The internet generation sometimes acts as though everything progressive or alt was invented since 2010."

Still, she insists there's plenty of room on the broom for everyone, but does suggest those who want to use the term and embrace the community go deeper. "I would encourage them to think about what attracts them to it. Is it sisterhood? Spirituality? The opportunity for activism? And then I'd say read books, follow blogs and delve into the history."

The Spell of *Social Media*

Online platforms are bringing witches from around the world out of the broom closet.

Ash Krafton is a *USA Today* bestselling author and hedge witch, who pens her speculative novels from a quaint cottage tucked away on a dead-end road in the middle of a Pennsylvania cornfield. While she may have a dearth of actual neighbors, Krafton enjoys combining her solitary practice with fellow witches via the online pagan community. "How else could I learn, if not for the internet?" she asks. "It's not like Barnesville has a school for it."

Instagram, online videos and audiobooks have been a huge help, she explains: "[They] give me a sense of being with another person of the same mind, and give me more validity than it would if I were reading silently."

She's hardly alone. Interest in the craft has been brewing online since the advent of the internet, though Krafton feels "COVID-19 really boosted the signal." After centuries shrouded in secrecy, witches around the world are stepping into the spotlight on platforms

ASH KRAFTON

Erin Harker created The Magick Makers (themagickmakers.com) as a space "that encourages and supplies your magickal practice at home."

"During the pandemic especially, people found comfort in my content," says Lilith Astrology founder Adama Sesay. "I do group online sessions, moon circles and classes so people can connect."

SABRINA SCOTT

"THE INTERNET BECAME CRUCIAL FOR FINDING KINDRED SPIRITS AND PEOPLE WITH SIMILAR BELIEFS."

❧ *Sabrina Scott*

like Facebook and YouTube. The hashtag WitchesofInstagram is connected to 6.5 million posts, while over at TikTok, a quick search for #WitchTok finds nearly 11 *billion* posts. Social media is clearly under the spell of witchcraft.

The allure is that these platforms offer a community to gather and learn regardless of location. As Erin Harker, the North Carolina–based founder of The Magick Makers, a store for the modern witch, explains, "Many of us have felt like outliers most of our lives, and the witch community online has opened up a whole world of people who walk similar paths."

That community is a lot more diverse than some mainstream outlets would suggest. One of the first witches to enchant Instagram was Bri Luna, best known as The Hoodwitch. She has amassed nearly 500,000 followers and is verified for sharing educational tarot card explanations, mantras and pictures of crystals and candles, under the tagline: "Everyday magic for the modern mystic." Luna, who is Black and Mexican, has given the world a peek inside the reality of witchcraft in the 21st century for the past decade in the form of her nearly daily posts. She is a true pagan pioneer, who told *Cosmopolitan* she felt inspired

to create The Hoodwitch because of how witches had long been represented. "[The] aesthetic was very white, very Salem, very *American Horror Story: Coven*. It was all dark robes and pointy hats." Luna helped usher in a new generation of tech witches and magical influencers including Harmony Nice, Pythian Priestess, Divine Mysticz and The Witch of Wanderlust.

"Social media has had an integral role in making these communities more accessible to everyone," agrees Adama Sesay, founder of Lilith Astrology (lilithastrology.com), who uses her accounts to interact with clients and explore aspects of the metaphysical. "There are so many more diverse voices; it's much more reflective of the

MICHELE LEFLER

community. In the past there were only a few people putting things out there, but now there is something for everyone."

OLD MEETS NEW

Indeed, navigating the witch world has never been easier, thanks to our smartphones and limitless-data plans.

"The past year has been especially tough with so many folks isolated…and the world apparently going mad around them; one of the easiest resources is to stare into the black mirror in your hand and try to dial up some sort of relief," says Jason Myers, founder of the band Icarus Witch and a social media marketing executive. "Most witches I know have a thirst for arcane knowledge and a desire to share ideas with others of like mind."

Case in point: Annabel Margaret, known as The Green Witch to her nearly 300,000 YouTube followers, is famous for her enchanting videos that range in topic from how to cast a calm spell to a recipe for a natural, healing lip salve.

While Margaret is showcasing ancient techniques via current technology, Maren Altman embraces a much more modern niche; she combines her astrology practice with market-charting focused on cryptocurrency. "I am never going to tell someone to buy this or that," the New York City–based witch says. "I can predict price trajectories, but I do not claim to be a financial adviser."

Social media also provides the perfect platform for expanding and enhancing practices. "Users can freely obtain information about the craft with just a few keystrokes—that kind of knowledge could have taken previous generations months to track down," says Myers. "Whether you're a baby witch, a solitaire seeking cyber companions or an elder looking to stay in touch with people, social media presents a multitude of methods to connect and feel a sense of communal belonging."

It's opened up learning possibilities for those far away from major cities. "Online spiritual communities can be a beautiful thing," says Sabrina Scott, who offers tarot readings and classes to her more than 11,000 Instagram followers (@sabrinamscott). "Technology has really expanded my ability to teach witchcraft and magic. I actually feel closer to my magic students online than I have when teaching in person."

Virtual covens are trendy, for sure, but there are also options for solo practitioners seeking a friendly face. "Not all witches are part of a coven...but that doesn't mean all solitaries prefer to be alone 100% of the time," says Michele Lefler of Living Moon Meditation (livingmoonmeditation.com). "I'm

> **"THERE ARE AS MANY WAYS OF UTILIZING SOCIAL MEDIA FOR WITCHCRAFT AS THERE ARE TYPES OF WITCHES."**
>
> *Jason Myers*

a Jewish witch and blend witchcraft into my Judaism. There aren't many 'jewitches' around where I live. There are quite a few of us out there, though, and social media has helped me find others who practice in similar ways to me."

Plus, it opens doors for the shy witch-curious. "Certain types of introverts feel freer to express their true nature in virtual reality," notes Myers. "When we're inhibited by the anxiety that can accompany being in a circle with people in real life, [virtual interactions] may open up more energy."

UNITY & UNDERSTANDING

Just glancing at what others are up to can be eye-opening. Says Lefler, "I see

many witches sharing spells and rituals and tips. When you need inspiration for adding some new magic to your space, it's fun and easy to turn to social media to see what other witches are doing."

Myers also uses social media for meditation. "I partake in online rituals with various covens or groves and enjoy daily meditation though apps," he says.

Of course, a subject as misunderstood as witchcraft is bound to attract online scuffles. "Since the pandemic hit, haters and trolls have been off the charts. Even within the community—witches lashing out at other witches," says Scott. She tries to immediately block negativity: "It's my own safe space to be creative."

Then there's the misinformation. "There is still a lot of bad intel out there about witchcraft; it doesn't always need to be your battle to counteract that," says Myers. "If you continue to put positive, truthful energy out, you'll often find the law of attraction will put you in the presence of those who may illuminate your path." And the good far outweighs the bad. "I've seen social media normalize the craft in many ways," says Myers. "It's helped ease the stigma for many who otherwise may have only associated witchcraft with the sensationalized tropes Hollywood has been pushing for generations rather than seeing it for what it actually is: a modern, nature-based spirituality path that espouses harming none, self-empowerment and environmental stewardship." Lefler agrees: "It shows we aren't devil worshippers with green faces and warts. Social media has been great for getting the word out that witches are normal people, just like everyone else." —*Amy L. Hogan*

"Social media is a great way to build your network of witches," says Jason Myers of the band Icarus Witch (icaruswitch.com).

Dressing the Part

Basic black and a high hat are always in vogue!

1. Mariah Carey at a party. 2. Meryl Streep as the Witch in *Into the Woods*. 3. 1940s pinup girl Peggy Ryan. 4. Mary-Kate and Ashley Olsen in *Double, Double, Toil and Trouble*. 5. Angelina Jolie in *Maleficent*. 6. Elizabeth Montgomery as Samantha Stephens on *Bewitched*. 7. Melissa Joan Hart as Sabrina Spellman on *Sabrina the Teenage Witch*. 8. 1940s pinup girl Adele Jergens. 9. Jamie Lee Curtis at a party. 10. Maleficent in Disney's *Sleeping Beauty*. 11. Cher's farewell tour. 12. Suzanne Somers in a witch costume. 13. Mayim Bialik in *Blossom*. 14. Candice Bergen as Shirley Schmidt on *Boston Legal*. 15. Margaret Hamilton as the Wicked Witch of the West in *The Wizard of Oz*. 16. Maggie Smith as Professor McGonagall in *Harry Potter*. 17. Lucille Ball on *I Love Lucy*. 18. Mother Goose. 19. Anjelica Huston as the Grand High Witch in *Witches*. 20. Author Sybil Leek. 21. Laurie Cabot, the official witch of Salem. 22. Sigourney Weaver at a party. 23. Cassandra Peterson as Elvira. 24. 1920s pinup girl Bessie Love. 25. Bette Midler at a party. 26. Jennifer Garner trick-or-treating. 27. The Evil Queen in Disney's *Snow White & the Seven Dwarfs*. 28. Randy Marsh on *South Park*. 29. 1960s pinup girl Karen Jensen.

Demystifying the Look

Traditional witch attire casts an enchanting spell.

HAT

The most recognizable part of Halloween witch wear, the conical black hat has disputed origins. One theory is it comes from the "Subeshi Witches"—three female mummies from the second century who had hair covered by black funnels. Another hypothesis: In the 1200s, the Catholic church required Jews to wear a pointed cap; as many Jews were accused of black magic, the hat took on the association. A similar theory suggests Puritans feared cap-wearing Quakers. One more origin possibility: The hats were worn by alewives—female beer brewers—who were accused of witchcraft by men in the industry. No matter the origin, they have been firmly associated with the witch since L. Frank Baum's *Oz* books featured hat-wearing witches in 1900.

BLING

For many witches, jewelry is more than decorative. Crystals and gems like moonstone, amethyst, bloodstone and various quartz types are believed to have different powers that can offer the wearer prosperity or protection. Celtic knots and loops—symbolizing the interconnectedness of life—as well as the pentagram are also popular and pretty.

BROOMSTICK

The association of the witch and the broom goes back to ancient pagan traditions, where the broom is thought to be a balance of masculine energies, represented by the handle, and the feminine energies of the bristles. The sweeping tools were often used to cleanse an area before a ritual. As to why witches fly on their broomsticks? Historians such as David Kroll posit the broom handle was used to apply hallucinogenic herbal balms—witches' brews, if you will—to the skin; the flying was likely just the high.

BLACK DRESS

The hue is always in fashion, but it is particularly popular for witches, whether it's a skintight sheath or flowing robe. "Black is the culmination of all vibrational rates of light on the material plane," Laurie Cabot, the official witch of Salem, has said (she notes actual witches wear many colors). "Black absorbs light information and helps witches be more receptive to psychic impressions and energies."

WAND

Wands and witches go all the way back to "The Odyssey," where witch-goddess Circe uses one to turn Odysseus' men into pigs. They've been written about in multiple books on magic, and of course are favorites of Oz's Glinda, Narnia's White Witch and many a fairy godmother. "Magic wands are used in healing and for directing energy," Cabot has said.

CAT

Some ancient cultures thought black cats were gods or good-luck symbols, but in the Middle Ages, the dark feline became associated with witches and evil. Cats are most active at night, which is when people feared witches worked their dark skills. Some believed the animals were carrying out a witch's bidding, while others thought they were spirit guides. While shelters still have trouble placing them, black cats make lovely pets for witches and nonwitches alike.

GUCCI

CHANEL

ANDREW GN

CHANEL

JULIEN FOURNIÉ

ROKH

CRAFT HAUTE COUTURE

From medieval corsets to whimsical capes, high-fashion brands like Valentino and Chanel have released collections inspired by witches. "I have always found witches stimulating," noted French designer Julien Fournié, who called one of his recent collections "First Spell." "Haute couture and magic share a taste for accumulated experience and tricks of the trade."

NOIR KEI NINOMIYA

ELIE SAAB

VALENTINO

VIKTOR&ROLF

ANNA SUI

JULIEN FOURNIÉ

SIMONE ROCHA

△

GETAWAYS

Make an *Escape*

*You don't need a flying broomstick
to visit these places steeped in the history
and culture of the craft.*

THE SALEM WITCH MUSEUM

SALEM, MASSACHUSETTS

Perhaps no place in the world is more associated with witches than this site of the infamous Salem witch trials in the 1690s. (For more, see page 36.)

For a broad overview, start at *The Salem Witch Museum*, 19½ Washington Square North. One section features exhibits detailing the witch hysteria and its tragic outcome, while a second wing explores how the perception of witches has changed over time (salemwitchmuseum.com). For more on the culture and history of the town itself, check out *The Salem Museum* at 32 Derby Square (thesalemmuseum.org). Then head to *The House of the Seven*

95

Gables at 115 Derby Street. Nathaniel Hawthorne wrote his famed Gothic novel of the same name after spending time with his family at this spooky site, then called the Turner-Ingersoll Mansion. Originally built in 1668, it's open to the public and offers insight into the author's world, as well as history about Judge John Hathorne, Nathaniel's great-grandfather (the writer is rumored to have changed the spelling to distance himself) and a particularly punitive player in the trials (7gables.org).

To learn about another overzealous overseer of the trials, visit *The Witch House,* 310½ Essex Street. The only remaining structure in Salem with direct ties to the trial, this 17th-century manse was the home of Judge Jonathan Corwin. Visitors can walk on the old floorboards and view artifacts and reproductions from the period (thewitchhouse.org).

You can pay your respects at the *Salem Witch Memorial*, 24 Liberty

SALEM WITCH MEMORIAL BENCHES

BEWITCHED STATUE

THE WITCH HOUSE

Up in Flames

The Great Salem Fire of June 1914 burned for days, destroying 1,400 buildings and leaving half the town homeless and jobless. Legend says it was started by the ghost of accused witch Giles Corey, who was pressed to death in 1692.

HOWARD STREET CEMETERY

97

GRAVES AT THE REBECCA NURSE HOMESTEAD

Street, which consists of 20 granite benches—each bearing the name of one of the accused—forming a stone wall around the Old Burying Point. Or explore *The Howard Street Cemetery*, 29 Howard Street, one of the primary burial grounds associated with the witch trials.

There's no shortage of tours and shows designed to scare and astound with varying degrees of tackiness. In the top-rated *History & Hauntings of Salem* two-hour walking tour, a licensed guide sheds light on the city's lore; go at night for a darker version (viator.com). And fans of 1960s TV should obviously check out the **Bewitched** *statue* of Elizabeth Montgomery as alter ego Samantha Stephens astride a broom in *Lappin Park*.

DANVERS, MASSACHUSETTS

While parts of Salem can seem a bit touristy or disrespectful, a 15-minute ride to Danvers, Massachusetts

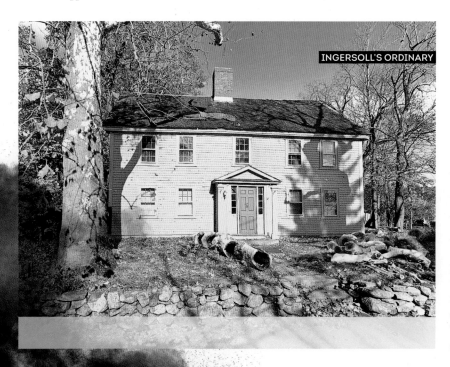

INGERSOLL'S ORDINARY

(formerly Salem Village), can be a more solemn and personal experience. The *Tercentennial Witchcraft Victims Memorial* at 176 Hobart Street opened in 1992 on the 300th anniversary of the trials and features haunting and heartbreaking quotes from many of the accused.

Down the road at 199 Hobart, take a peek at *Ingersoll's Ordinary*, a former tavern where accused witches were held in the upstairs rooms and officials and spectators ate and drank during the proceedings.

You can book a guided tour at the *Rebecca Nurse Homestead* at 149 Pine Street and hear the story of Nurse, a beloved 71-year-old church member who was convicted and executed despite public outcry (rebeccanurse.org).

At 67 Centre Street, you'll find the path of the *Salem Village Parsonage*, where the witch hysteria first began in 1692, when the Rev. Samuel Parris' daughter and niece first became "afflicted" from witchcraft. Then follow the historic plaques.

THE TERCENTENNIAL
WITCHCRAFT VICTIMS
MEMORIAL

LANCASHIRE, U.K.

Though largely Protestant, England still has a sad history with witch trials, most famously the 1612 conviction and hanging of 10 accused witches from Pendle. More than half of the accused came from two rival families helmed by aged widows—Elizabeth Southerns (aka Old Demdike) and Anne Whittle (called "Mother Chattox" for her clicking teeth). Both women made money advertising themselves as witches and healers (something not uncommon in village

LANCASTER CASTLE

THE FOUR ALLS INN

GAWTHORPE HALL

PENDLE HERITAGE CENTRE

life at the time), and scholars believe it was their competition that led to cross-accusations and tragedy. A full account can be found in *The Wonderful Discoverie of Witches in the Countie of Lancaster*.

In commemoration of the 400th anniversary of the trial, a 51-mile footpath (for walkers or drivers) was built from **Barrowford** to **Lancaster** following the route the accused were likely to have walked. Ten tercet way-markers (one for each victim) along the trail each contain a verse comprising the poem "The Lancashire Witches" by U.K. poet laureate Carol Ann Duffy. The path begins with the **Pendle Heritage Centre**, Colne Road, Barrowford, Burnley, which features a museum and garden (pendleheritage.co.uk). Stops through the Pendle Forest include: **Ashlar House**, where members of both the Chattox and Demdike families were questioned, and **Gawthorpe Hall**, which was a home to the landlords of two of the

A Pendle Panhandler

In March 1612, John Law refused beggar Alizon Device. He then fell ill (likely a stroke) and claimed to be a victim of Device's witchcraft. She confessed and implicated her grandmother, Old Demdike, and others.

accused and is said to be haunted. And there is **The Four Alls Inn**, where one of the Chattoxes allegedly turned the beer sour and bewitched her landlord's son (the current pub on the site is not the original and was built in the late 1700s).

The path ends at **Lancaster Castle**, where the trials took place. Accused witches weren't the only ones to meet a sad end here; Catholics and other religious minorities were sentenced to death as well. The castle was decommissioned as an operating courthouse in 2012, and now functions as a historic site, with guided tours (lancastercastle.com).

LALAURIE MANSION

HISTORIC VOODOO MUSEUM

NEW ORLEANS

There's a strong case to be made that New Orleans, with its multicultural traditions of Voodoo and Catholicism, is the true U.S. capital of magic.

Embrace the lore of Voodoo queen Marie Laveau (for more, see page 50). Head to *Louis Armstrong Park* and check out *Conga Square*, where Laveau famously led interfaith and interracial (taboo at the time) dances and rituals in the 1800s. Her ghost has allegedly been spotted at her tomb in *St. Louis Cemetery No. 1*, as well as at the site of her home (the original building was torn down in 1903) at 1020 St. Ann Street.

For those looking for additional supernatural stories, many companies offer ghost tours highlighting Laveau's old haunts, as well as the dubious *LaLaurie Mansion*, where Madame Marie LaLaurie allegedly tortured and killed many of her enslaved people, and the *Hotel Monteleone*, where a young child died but reportedly his ghost reappeared to comfort his bereaved parents—and others.

You can learn more about traditional practices at the *Historic Voodoo Museum*, 724 Dumaine Street. Since 1972, this small moss-covered stop in the French Quarter has housed historic art and artifacts of the city's rich magic and mystery (voodoomuseum.com). There's also the *New Orleans Pharmacy Museum*, 514 Chartres Street. Established in 1823, this site offers a glimpse into historic treatments, many of which incorporated traditional folk remedies (pharmacymuseum.org).

And there are few places in the world with more shops selling crystals, amulets, herbs and poppets (dolls). Mediums will read your tarot cards, your palm or even place a hex on your enemy, which we don't recommend—rule of three and all!

BLÅ JUNGFRUN ISLAND, SWEDEN

Legend has it this remote granite island—also known as "Witches' Mountain"—was the spot where witches convened with the devil on Maundy

LOUIS ARMSTRONG PARK

TROJEBORG ON BLÅ JUNGFRUN ISLAND

Thursday. The story goes it was only accessible by magical flight, and for years offerings were left on the beach in hopes of reaching and appeasing any otherworldly beings who lived there.

Those 15th-century legends might not be all wrong. In 2014, archaeologists discovered evidence that ancient humans lived in the caves; among the findings were artifacts including altars, suggesting they engaged in ritualistic practices.

Currently, the island is a national park with lush deciduous forests, a wide variety of rare beetles and birds, and a somewhat creepy *Trojeborg*—a stone labyrinth. A broomstick or private plane is no longer needed to get there; a local boating company ferries passengers out for a three-and-a-half-hour tour multiple times a week.

While the stones might be pretty, resist the temptation to take one as a souvenir, because legend says if you remove a rock from the island, you'll be cursed for eternity (nationalparksofsweden.se).

103

THE BANDILAAN
MOUNTAIN VIEW PARK

OLD BALETE TREE

SIQUIJOR, PHILIPPINES

Back in the 1600s, Spanish colonists dubbed this island in the central Philippines "The Island of Fire" because it gave off an eerie glow from thick swarms of fireflies. Others gave it the moniker the "Island of Witches" because of the magical practices of locals.

Now, 400 years later, it still has a strong tradition of the mystic, with healers known as "mananambals"who mix herbal remedies for whatever ails you. Each spring in *The Bandilaan Mountain View Park*, they hold a large festival after weeks of collecting herbs. Visitors can buy potions for love and health and everything in between (pia.gov.ph).

Just west of the village of Campalanas, visitors can admire the massive *Old Balete Tree*. Said to be 400 years young, it's supposedly a site of ancient rituals and home to mythical fairies, demons and elves. We can't guarantee you'll see those, but a natural spring-fed pool at the tree's long roots is full of little fish that will happily nibble dead skin from your feet.

Of course, you can also enjoy the excellent snorkeling, gorgeous forests and top-notch resorts!

LA PAZ, BOLIVIA

Forget your local new age shop. Those interested in a truly epic assortment of witchy goods should head to *El Mercado de la Brujas and La Hechiceria*—which translates into "The Witches Market"—located in the *Cerro Cumbre* mountain clearing in La Paz. Black-hat-wearing witch doctors known as "Yatiri" offer all manner of talismans, amulets, potions and herbs. Among the most popular items are dried llama fetuses, which are planted under homes as an offering to a fertility goddess.

EL MERCADO DE LA
BRUJAS IN LA PAZ

HEXENTANZPLATZ

On the Watch

In the small German villages near the Brocken, visitors will find cobbled streets and historic half-timbered houses, many dating back to the Middle Ages, and...witches! Residents and shops often decorate their lawns and stoops with life-size straw, stone or wooden witches.

HARZ MOUNTAINS, GERMANY

Witches have long been associated with the **Brocken**—the highest point in Germany's Harz Mountain range. Legends tell how they made sacrifices to Norse gods and celebrated Walpurgisnacht (witches' night), something Johann Wolfgang von Goethe immortalized in his tragedy *Faust*.

The 62-mile footpath known as the **Harz Witches' Trail** runs from Osterode through the mountains, or to make it easier you can just hop on the **Brocken Railway** to the **Harz National Park and Botanical Garden**. Here, you can learn about history in the museum, admire the witch and demon statues at a plateau known as the **Hexentanzplatz** ("the devil's dance

floor"), and then follow **The Goethe Way**, a trail to the peak that the author took in 1777. But don't get spooked by the famed **Brocken Spectre**—the way your shadow is made long and creepy by the mist.

On April 30, Brocken is the epicenter of the beloved annual Walpurgisnacht celebration, observed throughout Scandinavia and Europe. Thousands of reveling witches and their crews "storm city hall" in the neighboring towns of *Thale* and *Goslar*, celebrate pagan traditions, build epic bonfires, drink all means of brews, and hike up the side of the mountain. In the words of Goethe: *Now, to the Brocken, the witches ride!*

BROCKEN'S SUMMIT

CHAPTER 3

EXPLORING YOUR INNER WITCH

*PRACTICING WITCHES OFFER ADVICE ON HOW TO GET
IN TOUCH WITH YOUR OWN POWERFUL MAGIC.
LEARN THE BASICS OF SPELL WORK WITH A CASTING PRIMER,
AND DISCOVER THE LONG-STANDING CONNECTION
BETWEEN CREATIVITY AND THE CRAFT.
PLUS, AN A-TO-Z LOOK AT ALL THINGS WITCHY.*

Listening to the Magic Within

You don't need a lot of fancy tools or exotic aids to make a connection with your inner witch.

> ❉ "The more you put into your relationship with the Earth, the more you get out of it," says author Paige Vanderbeck.

I am the author of two books of spells, rituals and practices, as well as the editor of *Luna Luna Magazine*, a space for magic and literature. But I'd be lying if I didn't tell you my path to magic was nonlinear. The road was paved with doubt, changing beliefs and life traumas that made it hard for me to feel anything remotely magical. There were also

times I was frightened to peer into the abyss, where mystery and intuition and personal power live—but I'm so happy I did.

Although I consider myself a *word witch* these days (I use writing as a way of making magic), I didn't realize I was already a witch, just because I *felt* like one. For a long time, I thought I needed permission from someone older

and wiser, or access to archaic occult information, and of course expensive tools. After all, books I'd read required special herbs (like rue!) or tools (like an athame, or blade)—things I couldn't get my hands on.

Here's the truth: You don't *need* tools or permission to tap into your own magic. You simply need to connect to that effervescent, wild spark within you—the part that feels connected to energy and attracted to the magical.

Everyone's path looks different, but in general all you need is a dedication to learning, intention and a respect for the lineage of the witch.

BE OPEN TO MYSTERIES

When I was about 12, I discovered a book about fairies at the local library, and I'd fall into its pages for hours. I would plant myself on the slick, algae-covered rocks that sat in the trickling bend of the river running behind my house, and I'd look for them.

Something pulled me to the fairies' mythos; mostly, it was the idea that they could only be glimpsed if you believed. If you knew where to look, you might find them sparkling in the summer light. I wanted so badly to peer beyond the scrim of this world.

To me, nature was a place of mystery— where the flora, fauna and water offered messages. I was *so young*, but I felt it. I'd always had this innate interest in what couldn't be seen but could be felt or intuited. And I leaned into that.

Even though there are lots of "magical" things that can't be proven— think spirits or crystals for healing— it's precisely that surrendering to the unknown that creates a life of magic. Being curious about the natural world, and open to the mysteries around us, is what opens the door to your inner witch.

There is no true right or wrong in starting your path. You can call on gods, deities, ancestors or simply your higher self. You can cast spells or not. What matters most is tuning in to yourself and the world around you.

EMBRACE THE ARCHETYPE

If you are pulled to spell craft, or if you want to connect to the intuitive, sexual, inclusive archetype of the witch, explore it. Visit your local library or indie bookshop and peruse the witchcraft section. Here's my advice: Grab the book that calls out to *you*. Read the one that makes your intuition sit up and listen. Run your fingers along the spines of each volume, giving your body the space and trust to feel the one that is right for *you*.

As Gaby Herstik, author of *Inner Witch*, says, "Spend an afternoon looking through books, writing down key words and phrases that resonate with you, and then find their common connections. Whether you like crafting, cooking, herbs, tradition or otherworldly entities, you can always incorporate your passions into your spell work and magic."

As I personally got deeper and deeper into learning about witchcraft, I gave myself permission to be carried into the depths. Eventually, I found that the universe led me to certain books or places or things that could help me grow. That's the mystery at play. There were some books that explored paths that didn't speak to me—and that's OK.

Beyond learning about a specific kind of magic, you'll want to dive into the history of the witch. She is a misunderstood, shamed, blamed and divisive figure who has been reduced to either villain or vixen or simplified by Instagram aesthetics. Witches are complex and have no fixed definition.

As Pam Grossman, author of *Waking the Witch*, has said, "There is also a chance that she is *you*, and that 'witch' is an identity you have taken upon yourself for any number of reasons—heartfelt or flippant, public or private."

Part of embracing the witch is also recognizing what practices belong or

JOURNALING YOUR WAY TO THE WITCH

As you move through your journey of discovery, you may want to keep a journal or book of shadows. Jot down any coincidences, dreams, feelings, realizations or themes that keep cropping up.

SOME PROMPTS:

- The witch represents ___ to me.
- What does magic mean to me?
- The natural element I feel most connected to is ___.
- I dreamed about ___ and I believe these symbols mean ___.
- I am tapping into my intuition by ___.
- Which books are speaking to me, and why?
- Which moon phase makes me feel extra powerful?
- The intention I want to live by is ___.

do not belong to you. Respect practices from closed cultures; these should only be embraced by people from that culture. Do some research if something calls out to you and make sure it's yours to practice. Learn about the history of the witch, and ask yourself: *What stands out to me about these stories?*

BUILD A RELATIONSHIP WITH THE NATURAL WORLD

Paige Vanderbeck, author of *Green Witchcraft* and host of The Fat Feminist Witch podcast, says, "Your connection to the natural world grants you access to the energy all around you for spiritual purposes, but it also helps you tap into the magic inside you."

So get into nature. Notice how your body changes: Does your heartbeat settle? Does your anxiety decrease? Do the trees—in their old age and wisdom—inspire you to find perspective and pause?

The witch respects and honors the medicine and magic of nature, so spend some time in your local park or backyard. Sit on the ground and feel the energy of the Earth (and below the ground, all the way into the center of the Earth) connecting with you, surging up through your spine. Notice how it grounds and energizes you.

You'll also want to develop a relationship to the moon, for she is a guiding light (both literally and proverbially) for witches. She symbolizes intuition, psychic power, emotional vulnerability and magic. But more so, she reminds us of the life-death-rebirth cycle.

Witches also work by the light of the moon or time their spells to different moon phases (waxing, waning, full).

Find a moon-phase app and take notice of the lunar cycle; journal about your feelings during each phase. Do you feel a certain way during the full moon? What about when the moon is waning, that time when the light is disappearing from the night sky?

CREATE A SPACE

It's important you return to your magic daily. Grossman recommends creating a sacred space for yourself: "Whether that is an altar or a shelf or a corner of a windowsill, it should be dedicated to connecting to the divine. A space where you don't put your cellphone or your keys, but you put sacred objects—photos of your ancestors, flowers, stones—whatever symbols help you feel connected to spirits."

Think about the things that make you feel connected to the Earth, to magic or to your own inner power—and create a space where you go and feel inhabited by that energy. This might be a place where you meditate, leave letters to gods or your higher self, or where you repeat an affirmation each morning. Perhaps this is where you'll practice spell work. But here, even the simplest acts engage the sacred.

"Being conscious and aware of your thoughts, of what you believe, of the way you talk to yourself, of the way you spiral or the way in which you distract yourself from your thoughts, is vital," Herstik has said. "To be powerful witches, we need to work with the mind and not against it."

LISA MARIE BASILE *is a poet and writer and is the author of several books, including* Light Magic for Dark Times *and* The Magical Writing Grimoire.

"BY STUDYING AND WORKING WITH NATURAL ELEMENTS LIKE PLANTS, CRYSTALS AND THE COSMOS, WITCHES BECOME IN TUNE WITH CYCLES OF GROWTH, EVOLUTION, HARMONY, LIFE AND DEATH."

— *Author Paige Vanderbeck*

Practicing mindfulness, like deep breathing and meditation, can help harness your energies.

the A B C of Spell Work

A longtime witch provides the basics for starting your own magical practice.

One thing many of those who call themselves witches have in common is the belief that magic is real and can be used to create positive change. But for those starting out (or even those who have been practicing for a while), casting spells can be extremely confusing.

There are plenty of books on the subject, but they're hardly all in agreement, and some contain suggestions ranging from unhelpful to dangerous. Add the fact that not all witches approach spell work in the same way, and it is little wonder people sometimes find it hard to know where to begin. Here are the basics of how I do spell work, but it's hardly the only approach. Keep in mind, the only way to actually discover what works best for you is to practice.

ASK THE RIGHT WAY

Spells can be used for everything from protection from enemies to getting a promotion. But spell work for prosperity will not be exactly the same as spell work for healing; what is included in one spell often isn't in another. The one thing most spells have in common is they are usually asking for something.

Before you get to the actual casting, it's important to establish your goal. The more definitively you can identify what it is you hope to achieve, the better you will be able to choose the spell you need. Make sure you give serious thought to what it is you really want. It might be something small or something important. Either way, you'll want to choose your words carefully.

There is a tricky balance between being too vague in your goal—"Send

me money"—and being too specific: "Send me a job that earns me at least $50,000 a year where I don't have to talk to anyone ever." You want to be precise about what you want, while still leaving the gods room to fulfill your wishes in ways you might not have considered. (You wouldn't believe how many times this has happened to me!) One famous example: A witch asks for "Mr. Right" and then ends up meeting "Mr. Wright."

Here is a good example of a prosperity spell that strikes a balance between the specific and the general:

God and goddess, hear my plea
Rain prosperity down on me
Bring in monies large and small
To pay my bills, one and all
Money earned and gifts for free
As I will, so mote it be.

There are many great books out there with existing spells for every conceivable occasion, but you can also write spells yourself. It really isn't difficult, and

you shouldn't feel intimidated. Many people believe speaking in rhyme lends a spell more power, but it certainly isn't necessary, nor is using archaic words or flowery language.

Casting a spell can be as simple as standing in front of your altar (the space you've dedicated to your magical work) and speaking the words. It is, in many ways, the same as sending out a prayer. Anyone can do it. What makes spells

The Law of Similars

The basic premise here is like for like. Adding an object with a similar color, shape or characteristic of the desired goal during casting can strengthen a spell. For example, use a heart-shaped amulet when casting a love spell, or bandage the knee of a doll in a spell to help with joint pain.

Many witches believe their full power can be achieved in a defined circle.

THE FOUR ELEMENTS: WATER, EARTH, FIRE AND AIR

effective is the amount of focus and intent you bring, and the strength of the belief that powers it. If you don't believe what you're doing, you can hardly expect the universe to believe you.

AWARENESS & INTENT

The biggest concern I hear from new witches is that they will do a spell wrong and it will somehow backfire. This is a possibility; if a spell is powerful enough to create the outcome you want, it is also powerful enough to accidentally cause an outcome you don't. One of the best ways to avoid this is to choose your words—whether your own spell or someone else's—with awareness and intent.

Remember, your spell work doesn't take place in a vacuum. It's vital that no spell interferes with anyone's free will. While asking for love in general is perfectly fine, for example, I don't advise a spell aimed at a specific person. You wouldn't want someone to make you do something against your will, right? So why would you inflict your will on others?

I'm also against hexing or any other negative uses of magic. While there are people out there who feel such things are justified, I believe the law of returns (anything you put out comes back to you in threes) pretty much guarantees these kinds of spells will come back to bite you.

Sacred Circles

Many witches—especially those practicing in covens—perform magical work in a casting circle. For thousands of years, the circle has symbolized unity and protection, and many believe it forms a barrier to keep out unwanted energies. The circle may be physically marked or not, and there are many elaborate techniques to create a circle, but the most crucial part is always that participants define the space and truly believe in its borders.

If you are worried about doing accidental harm, add the following words to any spell: "For the good of all, and according to the free will of all."

A LITTLE ASSISTANCE

When doing their spell work, many witches call on the god and goddess (from some Wiccan and pagan traditions). Others choose to invoke a specific deity, either one they follow or one who is especially suitable for the work at hand, like Brigid for healing, or Venus for love. You can also call on the universe in general.

It is perfectly acceptable to read or recite your spell without any kind of ritual attached, especially if it is a spell for something simple. You can stand in front of your altar, or out under the full moon, and if you are speaking from the heart, that is enough. Many witches never do anything more complicated.

If the issue is important, or if you feel your spell work needs some extra oomph, you can use a few additional items to help focus your energy. I think of these things as part of a witch's tool kit, and they can include candles, gemstones, herbs, symbols, statues and

air, fire and water—or invoke the god and/or goddess. Place your magical tools on whatever you are using for an altar and focus on each one. Light a candle or candles, and drum or chant or meditate—whatever helps you focus your power. Many witches find it helpful to record their spells in a journal or book of shadows so they can document what works.

Keep in mind that even when you do everything right in casting your magic, there is never a guarantee your spell will work. While you can always ask, sometimes the answer might just be "no."

No matter how you go about it, know that spell work is a sacred and serious part of witchcraft, and should never be done lightly or just for fun. But if you do it correctly, it can add to your practice and bring positive energy into your life! —*Deborah Blake*

more. Some witches, including me, have quite the collection.

These tools are beautiful and fun, but they actually serve a purpose. Each element you add to your ritual serves to emphasize your goal and hone your focus. This can be especially helpful for those witches who are just starting out.

If you want to get more complicated, you can do some (or all!) of the following before casting the spell: Cleanse yourself and your magical space (sage or salt and water are good for this). Cast a circle that creates a place set aside from the mundane world. Call in the four elements—earth,

THERE'S A STONE FOR THAT

MANY WITCHES USE VARIOUS CRYSTALS TO ENHANCE THEIR SPELL WORK–AND THEY LOOK COOL, TOO!

CRYSTAL QUARTZ
If you can only have one stone, this is the one to get. Sacred to the goddess, it can be used to boost the energy of any spell and is good for protection, healing, and spiritual and psychic work.

AMETHYST
This purple stone is another all-around useful gem and is most commonly used for healing, love, peace, courage and happiness.

AGATES
These come in many colors, and you can pick one that is specific to the work you are doing, such as green for prosperity. They can be an inexpensive substitute for many other stones, and are good for protection, healing, love and courage.

LAPIS
This beautiful blue stone has been associated with power and magic in many cultures. Use it for love, healing, protection and joy, and to boost psychic abilities.

ROSE QUARTZ
A pink relative of crystal quartz, this is used for love, healing and peace.

TIGER'S EYE
This one works for just about everything, including prosperity, protection, courage and energy.

Feeling awed and inspired by the ocean? Even if you're landlocked, you can still use sea water (aka salt water) in your magic.

Creating
Sacred Spaces

Whether you have acres of land or a cramped city apartment, it's important to set up a designated place to disconnect from the world and perform magical work.

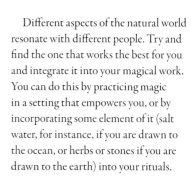

Many a witch and nonwitch alike has felt inspired by ancient sites like Stonehenge, in Wiltshire, England.

Having a sacred space is an important part of a witchcraft practice, just as it is for many other religious or spiritual paths. It's used for worship, as a place to connect with the gods or oneself, or as a safe area in which to practice magic.

What that means may vary widely from one person to another. A sacred space can be natural or man-made, simple or complicated, permanent or portable. As a witch, it's up to you to decide which forms of sacred space you wish to incorporate into your own practice. Keep in mind, one aspect of sacred space is that it sets you aside from the mundane world. Remember to turn off or leave your cellphone and electronic devices elsewhere, and try to set yourself up in a quiet place, where you won't be interrupted.

NATURAL SURROUNDINGS

For some, the most sacred spaces are those that are created by nature. I always feel the gods' presence very strongly at the ocean. Although I don't live anywhere near one, I try to make a pilgrimage at least once a year. I can sense the sacred in the movement of the waves and the sounds of the sea. Even when there are others around, the ocean is cleansing and empowering.

Walking through the woods and mountains gives me much the same feeling. There is an intrinsic, elemental power in trees and earth that can ground and reenergize you after too much time spent in the hectic modern world of electronics and constant noise. If you can't get to a forest, just sitting under a tree with your body in contact with the dirt underneath can help center you.

Different aspects of the natural world resonate with different people. Try and find the one that works the best for you and integrate it into your magical work. You can do this by practicing magic in a setting that empowers you, or by incorporating some element of it (salt water, for instance, if you are drawn to the ocean, or herbs or stones if you are drawn to the earth) into your rituals.

ANCIENT SITES

There are numerous sites throughout the world that are considered to be sacred both by those who live near them and those who journey to visit them. Stonehenge, for instance, is a famous sacred site that people travel to each year to observe the summer solstice. There are sacred mountains, such as Ararat in Turkey and Olympus in Greece, sacred water, like the Ganges River in India, ancient ceremonial sites, like Machu Picchu in Peru, and many more.

Some of these sites are considered sacred because of their locations on ley lines or other powerful conjunctions. Others may be sacred because they were used for ceremonies and worship over the course of many years, absorbing the energy of those who used them. A visit to one of these places is said to bring enlightenment, so they are definitely worth a trip if you can do it.

CREATING A SPACE AT HOME

For most of us, though, our magic is more likely to center around the sacred spaces we create in our own homes. Ritual circles and altars are at the core of a magical practice, and anyone can create one.

I personally have a number of sacred spaces at my house, although there has

been so much magic practiced on my property since I moved in almost 20 years ago, I now consider the entire place to be blessed and consecrated for magical work.

Out behind my barn, there's a permanent ritual circle with a fire pit in the center and stones marking its outer edges. I built it with my coven, Blue Moon Circle, the first year I lived there, and we have used it ever since. It is the traditional 9 feet across, and private enough that we can practice magic in peace. We have held many a Sabbat ritual there, cast spells and danced around the bonfire. But I live in upstate New York, where much of the year we're forced inside by inclement weather, so I also have areas inside that I use for magical work.

If we can't be outside for our group rituals, I have a round altar table that we set up in the middle of the living room. It's oak—one of the sacred woods—with sides that fold down so it can be put out of the way when it isn't in use. But you can use whatever you have.

For ritual, I cover the table with an altar cloth (I have a few different ones,

🌿 Magical objects can also act as decor.

depending on the season). Then I place a candle at each of the four quarters—north, east, south and west—along with a candle for the goddess at the full moons, or one each for the god and goddess if it is one of the Sabbats. The altar is then decorated with items appropriate to the occasion. Usually this includes crystals, fresh flowers or dried herbs, symbols of the season and any tools we'll need for whatever magical work we're doing that night. All these small touches help to focus our energy and remind us of our purpose.

We also always have a sage smudge stick, which we use for clearing and cleansing ourselves and the space when we start the ritual, as well as sea salt and a container of water, plus a small bowl to mix them in. We pass these around the circle for cleansing, too. This helps create intention for the area, as well as getting us into the right mental state.

In addition to the space I use when I practice magic with others, I have three altars set up around my house for when I need sacred space for myself. One, a shelf in the bedroom, is my cat altar, dedicated to the beloved companions

> **"MOST RITUAL WORK HAS TRADITIONALLY BEEN DONE IN A CIRCLE, IN PART BECAUSE OF THE EASE OF PRACTICE WITH OTHERS, AND IN PART BECAUSE THE CIRCLE SEEMS TO BE A NATURAL SHAPE FOR SPIRITUALITY."**
>
> ⚜ *Deborah Blake*

who have left this plane of existence. I have boxes with their ashes, pictures of the cats, cat figurines and other items that celebrate their lives. While it may be the most sacred spot in my entire home, it's only used for display, not for active magical work. Likewise, many people have ancestor altars dedicated to those who have passed, something which is a tradition in many different religions.

Most of my magical supplies are stored in a midsize cabinet in my dining room, the top of which is an altar I keep set up for simple spells. Above it is another handmade wooden cabinet with a glass front, where talismans and other magical tools are kept. I like the glass because being able to see the tools every day reminds me to connect to magic. If you live in a situation where you need to be more discreet, closed storage is fine.

But most of my magical work is done in front of a simple hand-carved wood shelf on my living room wall. This usually holds items that relate to whatever season it is, god and goddess figures, a wand I was gifted by a friend, some crystals and of course, candles. If I am going to do solitary magic, this is where I will stand. On my own, I rarely go through an entire ritual. Instead, I simply envision sacred space in my head, light a candle and cast the spell.

It's easy to create sacred space for yourself no matter where you live. Remember: Sacred space is mostly about your intention. Visualize yourself surrounded by a safe and blessed circle of light, cleanse it with sage or incense, sprinkle it with salt and water and feel yourself set apart from the mundane world. Or go stand with your feet in the surf or your arms around a tree. It's all about whatever feels sacred to you.

—*Deborah Blake*

CRYSTALS

ATHAME

Tools of the Trade

From herbs and candles to brooms and cauldrons, there is no shortage of aids to help you work your magic.

itchcraft is all about energy, intention, focus and belief. As long as you have those, you truly don't need anything else. That being said, many witches use tools, ranging from the purely practical to the decorative and beautiful. These items can be used to increase your focus and boost the energy of a spell, or they can act as symbols of a deity, a seasonal celebration or your magical intent. They can also be an empowering reminder of your identity as a witch.

There's a pattern to the type of energy associated with some common witchcraft objects. Tools that are upright and pointed generally represent masculine energies, while those that are cuplike or hollow are often associated with female

🌿 Most witches use the term herb to cover any plant, not just the ones we normally consider herbs, so your tool kit may contain anything from apple to yarrow.

DRUM

CHALICE

energies—witches aren't exactly subtle! These simply represent the basic male and female energies or deities, and can be used by anyone regardless of gender.

EXPLORING THE BASICS

Perhaps nothing is more closely associated with witches than the broom. Alas, I don't actually use mine for flying. Also known as a besom, the broom is generally used to sweep negative energy from a ritual space. Your magical broom should always be a special one, used only for that purpose, although it's fine to use a smaller version if you don't have room for a large version. The broom is the only magical tool representing both the male energies (the handle) and the female (the bristles).

An athame (AH-them-ay) is a double-sided magical knife often seen as a symbol of witchcraft. It is used to direct energy or to point (such as when pointing to the four quarters during a circle casting), but never to actually cut anything. They usually have a metal blade and a wooden handle, and can vary from basic to the ornate. The athame symbolizes the god and masculine energy.

Another pointing and energy-directing tool is the wand. Unlike in the movies, the wand has no intrinsic power, but is instead used to channel your own will. Wands are usually made of wood, and certain trees such as apple, oak and willow are considered particularly appropriate. A wand can also be made of metal or animal bone

CANDLES

Herbs such as sage, lavender and clove have multiple purposes in magical work. They can be burned as part of a ritual.

and decorated with anything from feathers to gemstones. Like the athame, it represents the male.

Two classic female/goddess tools are the cauldron and the chalice. The cauldron in particular is associated with the craft; people used to believe it was where witches created potions, probably evil ones. Keep in mind, however, that back in the early days, every household had a cauldron and they were more likely used for soup! Usually made of cast iron, although smaller ones might be made of copper or other metals, cauldrons come in all sizes—from miniatures that can fit in your palm to those large enough to hang over a fire or stand on their own on three legs. I have a small one to hold the sage we burn during ritual, and a larger version that we often fill partway with sand, then place tea lights or tapers in when can't be outside to have a bonfire.

The chalice is a cup or goblet that can be used to hold wine, water or any other liquid during magical work. It can be placed on an altar to represent the goddess. Chalices are often used during the "cakes and ale" portion of a ritual, and can be made of pottery, glass, metal or anything else you like. My group's chalice was crafted by one of our members, a potter, and decorated by all of us before she glazed and fired it. It's a treasured tool, because we all put a little of ourselves into it—but you certainly don't have to get that fancy.

CAULDRON

MORE MAGICAL AIDS

Some of my favorite tools are crystals (see page 115). A simple quartz is often placed on the altar on full moons to represent the goddess, although some people prefer moonstone or amethyst. Different stones are associated with different magical properties, and some witches (ahem, me) have extensive collections with gemstones for prosperity, protection, love and more. Luckily, many stones are multipurpose, so you can make do with just a few.

Candles are utilized for most rituals and spells, and may represent the god, goddess and the elements on an altar. They can also help focus the intent of a spell, such as using a green candle for prosperity. They're sometimes carved with rune symbols or anointed with magical oils to boost their power.

As long as there have been witches, they've been using herbs. Don't worry

WITCHCRAFT ON A SHOESTRING

DON'T HAVE THE MEANS OR DESIRE TO SHELL OUT A TON ON EXPENSIVE ACCOUTREMENTS? THAT DOESN'T MEAN YOU'LL HAVE TO PRACTICE SANS TOOLS. HERE ARE A FEW INEXPENSIVE OPTIONS FOR WITCHES ON A BUDGET.

WAND Simply find a smooth, reasonably straight stick about the length of your forearm (if you don't live in the woods, try a walk in a park). If you want, you can decorate it with feathers, draw rune signs on it or adorn it with pretty ribbons.

ATHAME Some inexpensive ones cost less than $10, but you need not spend even that. The main use of an athame is to point and direct energy; simply use your finger!

CAULDRON Large cast-iron cauldrons can be pricey. I found mine at a yard sale for a fraction of the cost. You can also substitute a small BBQ hibachi.

CHALICE A chalice doesn't have to be made of metal or fancy pottery. You can find a sturdy wine glass at the local dollar store. If you want, decorate it with glass markers.

CANDLES I love premade magical candles that come anointed with oils and etched with runes. But candles are one of the most inexpensive tools there are. You can buy simple white votives and dress them up with your own symbols by carving into the wax with a toothpick.

BOOK OF SHADOWS There are many beautiful BOS available to buy if you're so inclined. But if you're the slightest bit crafty, you can make your own by decorating a simple notebook or three-ring binder.

It can be fun and rewarding to create your own tools, and depending on how you go about it, a lot cheaper. If you work with a group, try having a ritual in which you create and then bless the tools you will use together. Remember: There is no one right way, and that whatever feels most appropriate probably is.

about having to track down exotic plants like mandrake root—most herbs can be found in the average kitchen. Even fancy potion ingredients like "eye of newt" are actually folk names for common herbs.

Like crystals, herbs have specific associations. Sage, for one, is often used for cleansing and clearing energy, which is why many witches use sage smudge sticks during ritual work. Just as with crystals, herbs are often multipurpose, such as basil, which can be used both for prosperity and protection.

How to keep track of all this? Books—and the gathering of knowledge in general—are essential to being a well-rounded witch. I have volumes on goddesses, crystals, herbs and the Sabbats, and that's not counting the ones I wrote!

Many witches record their practices with a book of shadows. Everyone does it slightly differently, but a BOS is generally used to write down spells and rituals, herbs and stones and their properties, and even recipes for feast food. These can be handmade or store-bought blank books, and are a perfect way to express your own witchy vibe.

There are plenty of other tools that add to the practice of magic, including drums and other instruments, pentacles (a five-pointed star representing the elements of earth, air, fire, water, and spirit, within a circle that stands for unity or the universe), incense, oils and divination tools like tarot cards, rune stones, scrying mirrors and even crystal balls.

Which of these you use is completely up to you. Pick ones that resonate with you and start with those. But if you end up with a hundred crystals, don't say I didn't warn you! —*Deborah Blake*

Otherworldly *Assists*

Tarot, astrology and similar tools are often shrouded in mystery and misconception. Here's the real deal.

It's a familiar scene in movies. Someone goes to see the psychic in her dramatic lair with beaded curtains and lunar decorations. No matter the tool—tarot cards, tea leaves, a crystal ball—the result is almost always the same: The psychic gasps in horror at what is revealed; the client is destined for some unspeakable fate, often so bad that the psychic will hurry the confused client out in great haste.

While that makes for great cinematic foreshadowing, it's a far cry from the way these tools actually work. "Sometimes people are scared of getting a reading because they believe it tells a preordained future, and they're afraid of getting bad news," says Mark Horn, a New York City–based tarot expert and author of *Tarot & The Gates of Light: A Kabbalistic Path to Liberation*. "I always explain that the cards [or another medium] don't tell the future—they help clarify the present so that you're better able to make choices about the future you want."

The "Wild Witch of the West," aka Rebecca M. Farrar, MA, a San Francisco Bay–area astrologer agrees, and claims these methods are really another form of self-discovery. "These are just tools to help connect you to the cosmos and a deeper understanding of yourself," she says. "A lot of people question themselves and their decisions, and these tools are a great way to mirror back and reflect."

PICK A CARD

Perhaps the most common tool for mystics is the tarot deck. Though some people claim the cards go back to ancient Egypt, most experts agree the illustrated tarot deck was developed in the 1400s as an Italian card game, and its mystic applications didn't really take off until around 300 years later, when people began using them for readings.

Though there are myriad different decks, the most influential and widely used is the Waite-Smith. First published by the Rider Company in 1909, it features

❀ Future events don't actually appear in the ball during crystal gazing. Readers instead claim that in concentrating on the ball, they can enter a trancelike state (not entirely different from meditation) that allows them to interpret images and events.

illustrations from Pamela Colman Smith drawn from the instructions of mystic and scholar A.E. Waite.

The deck is composed of 78 cards, but the most well-known are the 22 cards of the major arcana ("greater secrets"). These include The Fool, The Sun, The Devil, The Lovers and Death. For very general readings, the major arcana alone may be used, as these cards are said to represent the key themes and events in an individual's life.

The other 56 cards make up the minor arcana ("lesser secrets"), which deal with more everyday occurrences. These are divided into four suits—cups, wands, swords and coins or pentacles. For a complete reading they're often used in conjunction with the major arcana.

One of the biggest misconceptions people have is that the cards themselves are often ascribed mythical powers, with people believing they can summon spirits or cause fortune or misfortune, according to Misha Tuesday, a Michigan-based tarot expert and hypnotist who founded Hypno-Energize. "The cards are ink on paper, printed in factories, and if such things were possible it would be the practitioner doing it, not the cards," he says.

So what exactly do they do? The most basic answer: They cards can help you make decisions.

"Before a reading comes a question," says Horn. The most useful questions can't be answered with a simple yes or no, but instead leave room for discovery. "A good example of an open-ended question that isn't specific about a particular issue would be simply: 'What do I need to know?' That could be narrowed to 'What

"The major arcana show the soul's journey using symbols and archetypes," says tarot expert Mark Horn.

"AS FAR AS 'GOOD CARDS' AND 'BAD CARDS,' ALL CARDS HAVE MULTIPLE POSSIBLE INTERPRETATIONS, SOME DESIRABLE, SOME NOT SO MUCH SO."

❧ *Misha Tuesday*

do I need to know about my relationship with X?' or 'What do I need to know to advance in my career?' But asking 'Is there something blocking my advancement?' as a yes-or-no question leaves no room for exploring what the factors might be."

What happens if you have great questions and the cards reveal things like skulls and death and despair? "There are always cards that have images that can frighten people," says Horn, "but the cards are interpreted in the context of the spread and the question."

For example, one recent client asked Horn about their career, and the Ten of Swords came up—a card showing someone lying facedown on the ground with ten swords sticking out of their back. "It's certainly not a happy image, but looking at the cards around it, I told my client that the cards suggested they had chosen this career out of love, but that the reality of the last few years working at it had killed that love—and it was time to leave this career," says Horn. "This was a confirmation of what the client already knew inside, but was afraid to speak aloud until they saw it reflected back in the cards."

That idea, that the conclusions are already known on a subconscious level, is an important one to any of these tools. "I tell clients they already hold the answer to the question they come with, but sometimes they don't have access to

MISUNDERSTOOD MESSAGES

Perhaps the most widely known cards of the major arcana, Death, The Tower and The Devil also tend to be the ones that strike fear in the hearts of tarot newbies. ("Death" certainly has a scary ring to it.) But tarot expert Misha Tuesday explains that while these three cards might not give you the warm-and-fuzzies, there's actually nothing nefarious about them.

DEATH

THE TOWER

THE DEVIL

DEATH
"Death simply represents change. If you're attached to the way things were, it might be scary or painful because things aren't like that any more, but it doesn't mean literal death," says Tuesday. "Oftentimes, the Death card can be seen as permission to make positive changes."

THE TOWER
"The Tower is probably the hardest-edged major arcana," says Tuesday. "It represents destruction, chaos and things falling apart. The silver lining is that even when things go to sh*t, as they sometimes do, there will eventually be space to rebuild."

THE DEVIL
"The Devil card is often about unhealthy attachments or emotions like guilt and shame," says Tuesday, adding that it can actually lead to extremely positive change. "It can be a prompt to doing some introspection or even therapy to release that baggage."

that answer," says Horn. "It might be too threatening to their idea of themselves, or their relationship, so they push it into their unconscious. And that's where the cards excel—they show us what's going on beneath the surface and help us face inner truths."

Tuesday adds that no matter what is shown, nothing is set in stone. "While there are some harder cards that I usually call 'challenge cards,' there is no bad outcome because cards don't predict what will happen with certainty," he says. "I teach that it's unethical for readers to tell people that bad things will happen to them, because it takes away their agency—and in some cases can even lead to self-fulling prophecies."

BEYOND WHAT'S YOUR SIGN
Another common mystic tool to explore the self is astrology. At its most basic, this is the belief that the alignment of the stars, moons and planets at the time you were born has great impact on your mood, personality and life events.

Even the newest of mystic newbies probably knows their zodiac sign, but astrology is a lot more complex than simply claiming Scorpios are obsessive and competitive while the Aquarius-born are aloof nonconformists.

To get more accurate mappings, astrologers look beyond those zodiac symbols or "Sun Signs" to see what sign each planet was in when someone was born. They also examine the angles (the four cardinal points on an astrological chart) and the astrological "houses" (12 equal sections on the birth chart representing different facets of your life).

"A lot of people oversimplify and misunderstand the complexity," says Farrar. "They think, I know my sign and that's the whole story, but going beyond the sun sign is where things get interesting. When we overidentify with one part, we're rejecting other parts. And those parts that we're rejecting are the ones that can act up and give us problems."

Simply put, if you glance at your daily horoscope and find nothing resonates, it could be that you're putting too much focus on one thing—the sun sign. Farrar herself says she used to feel it was "stupid" until she began to seriously study archetypal astrology, and realized it was an "incredible tool for self-awareness." She suggests focusing on the angles of the planets in your chart as a good starting point.

"ASTROLOGY IS DESIGNED TO HELP YOU LEARN ABOUT YOURSELF AND YOUR PLACE IN THE WORLD; IT OFFERS TOOLS… TO NAVIGATE TIME AND OUR LIFE PURPOSE."

♣ *Emily Ridout*

Obviously you can't change the time of your birth, so how can having your whole astrological chart mapped out help you? Isn't this the kind of thing that's impossible to change? The answer is: not so much. "With astrology, the biggest misconception is that you are just your sign," says Emily Ridout, a Eugene, Oregon-based astro yoga specialist. "People think well, I'm a Libra so that's what I am. It's not. It's a map and this is a journey. The goal is

self-inquiry; gaining mastery of the self, and understanding your life force and how to use it. What you do with that information is up to you."

Ridout, who has studied multiple folklore traditions, claims astrology is a sister science to yoga, and often recommends yoga poses and practices to help someone based on their astrological chart. "I suggest activities to help people wake up parts of their chart so they can bring themselves into balance," she says. "It's about reminding you of something that is true and waking you up to it, so you can get back into alignment."

OTHER MYSTIC OPTIONS

There are plenty of other ways mystics seek guidance and self-actualization. For centuries, people have used tasseography, which has a querent looking for signs in the residue of tea leaves (or coffee grounds or wine sediments). Others are partial to palmistry—also known as palm reading or chiromancy—where users claim to find answers to pressing questions by studying the lines and shape of the palm. And some prefer crystal scrying or crystallomancy (looking into a crystal ball, à la Dorothy in *The Wizard of Oz*), where images can be interpreted to help make plans for the future.

All of these methods are open for self-exploration and need not have expensive barriers to entry. There is no shortage of books and online tutorials available, but the experts suggest it need not even be that formal. Simply looking at the cards of the tarot deck and examining how they make you feel, for example, has value.

If you would like help from an expert, it's not hard to find. Almost every city

❉ "Astrology shows you things you already know subconsciously," says astrologer Emily Ridout. "It's an act of remembering."

Palmistry has been practiced all over the world since ancient times. Although much attention (especially in movies) is often given to the life line, modern readers generally agree its length doesn't correspond with that of a person's literal life.

boasts storefront psychics with neon signs offering readings—sometimes for as little as a few bucks for a question. But be it tea leaves or tarot, if you're going to seek help from a professional, it's important to find someone whose methods gel with your goals. Some will be more theatrical, with elaborate rituals, while others offer more of an open dialogue. Above all, it's important you are comfortable with the person, and be on the lookout for obvious scams. "Avoid practitioners that are trying to be too mysterious or intense," says Tuesday. "The biggest red flag is someone who tells you that you are under a 'generational'-type curse and offers to do a cleansing ritual for a healthy fee."

And no matter how good your medium, keep in mind that she isn't a substitute for a licensed mental health practitioner.

What's Your *Path?*

Find out what type of witchcraft best fits your beliefs.

"The first thing you'll notice is that magic really changes you," says Wiccan priestess Phyllis Curott.

Witches have been around since before Biblical times, but one of the biggest appeals of the craft right now is its ability to be personalized. There's something for everyone in the world of witchcraft. "It's a spiritual practice that really suits the modern temperament," says Phyllis Curott, a Wiccan high priestess and author. "It can be incredibly nourishing for your soul and your life when you find [the sect] that resonates with your passions and curiosities and needs." There are myriad paths to choose; here are a few of the most popular.

CEREMONIAL

For those who like the structure and tradition of organized religion, ceremonial magic might be a good fit. Teachings are often derived from the early magic schools of the 1800s or before, but also incorporate scientific evidence. Study and rituals are more formal than in other pagan practices, and often involve specific tools and complex magic, such as communicating with spirits and healing.

COSMIC WITCH

Always staring at the stars? A cosmic practice could be your calling! These witches have been around since people began studying planets, and they tend to use astrology, astronomy and the cosmos in their rituals and spells. Planetary alignment, celestial energy and the zodiac are key elements for magical practices, which often honor celestial deities and raise energy. Meditation and birth charts are two popular tools.

❋ "Sometimes it's just nicer to have others to work with," says Wiccan Sandi Liss. "Working together raises the energy; multiple hands make for better or lighter work."

DIANIC

If feminism is your focus, the Dianic path delivers. In the 1970s, Z. (Zsuzsanna) Budapest created Dianic Wicca as a sacred space for women who wanted to practice their craft without men. This female-only sect, which was inspired by goddesses Artemis and Diana, focuses on goddess worship and the divine feminine. They honor the goddess and celebrate her creation of the web of life. Non-Wiccan Dianic paths have also gained popularity. But Dianic traditions are not without controversy—some covens have come under fire in recent years for denying transgender women entry.

DIVINATION

Dating back to ancient times, divination witches try to predict future events. Sometimes known as oracles, they've existed in almost every culture. Today, they may use tarot cards, tea leaves, *I Ching*, palmistry or other tools as their aids. Some diviners known as augurs believe spirits exist in everything in the natural world and can offer guidance. They may study everything from clouds, lightning and weather patterns to animals, insects and even human behavioral patterns. Though similar to a fortune-telling, augur practices are more formal and ritualistic.

ECLECTIC

A dash of this, a pinch of that! Eclectics draw from different traditions and cultures to create practices that suit specific needs and interests. Sometimes called nondenominational pagans, they may honor some deities from one sect, incorporate rituals from another and celebrate holidays from an entirely different tradition. Exploration and experimentation are freely encouraged. Because of its flexibility, this is probably the most common path found today. While many eclectics are solo practitioners, it's entirely possible to be a member of a coven.

ELEMENTAL

These witches honor the four elements: earth, fire, water and air, as well as the spirit that connects them. Often, they create a different altar for each of the elements and will call on one specifically when performing rituals or spell-casting. Many witches focus their practice on the element they feel most drawn to. An air witch may work with the wind and use tools such as a wand. Fire witches employ candles and bonfires. Earth witches have a penchant for grounding work, while water witches may look for signs in the sea or take ritual baths.

GREEN

If you hear music on the wind and see faces in the trees, you might just be a green witch. Skye Alexander, author of *The Modern Guide to Witchcraft*, calls them "the original tree-huggers," and says historically, green witches lived and worked apart from the community as herbalists, though today there are plenty of city or suburban green witches. Many people are drawn to this path because of a desire to help combat climate change. Green witches embrace all things Earth in their rituals and magic: plants, flowers, vegetation, rocks, crystals and wild-crafting. The goal is to feel as close to Mother Earth as possible.

HEDGE

Those interested in traveling to other dimensions may find happiness as hedge witches. Sometimes called astral witches, they focus on accessing the spirit world or "hedge jumping" into the otherworld. Their arsenal is stocked with herbs and crystals as they practice Earth-based magic, which helps them communicate with other realms. Some claim hedge witches "flying" into the spirit world is the origin of the witch on a broomstick. They also utilize plant medicine to heal the physical and spiritual woes.

+ TIME OF MAGIC +

❋ The four elements—earth, fire, water and air—as well as the planetary positions are important in many traditions.

HEREDITARY WITCH

Hereditary witches are born into the craft and perform magic that has been handed down from one generation to the next. "I practice the same folk magic that my mother and grandmother practiced," says Erin Moore, a midwife in Montana. No one is forced into it; even if your closest ancestors are witches, you must consciously opt to follow the path.

KITCHEN OR COTTAGE

If home is your oasis and you consider cooking a sacred art, you might be a kitchen or cottage witch. Both types tend to be loving, warm and welcoming. They see the magic in everyday life— even when cleaning and doing mundane chores. They often grow their own herbs for their rituals, potions and lotions and shine when cooking, brewing and baking. Kitchen witches utilize their own personal energy with oils, herbs and food, and basic household objects to make their magic. Cottage witches are less focused on food and more about the garden and foraging items to use in their healing remedies.

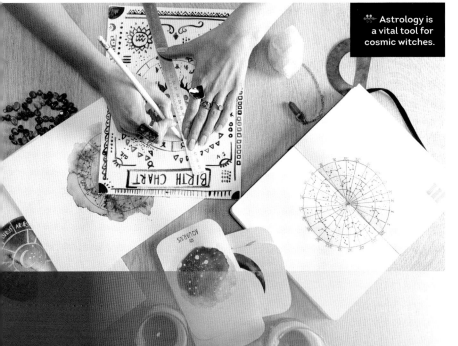

❋ Astrology is a vital tool for cosmic witches.

SEA WITCH

Do you feel most alive and at peace at the beach? You might be a sea witch. Unlike Ursula, who terrorized Ariel in *The Little Mermaid*, sea witches are usually peaceful people who use sand, shells and organic ocean matter in their practices. They feel an intense bond with water and see magic in everything that comes from the sea. They feel energized from the ocean and like luna (moon) witches, often study moon lore and perform their rituals in relation to tidal patterns.

SECULAR

Secular witches do not acknowledge the divine or spiritual, nor do they work with deities. Secular witches regularly incorporate oils, herbs, crystals and stones into their practices without any spiritual connection. They don't believe in objects having energy or that there is any energy in their practices. Interestingly, a secular witch can be a spiritual person, but their magic work is not spiritual in any way, shape or form.

SHAMANISM

A shaman embraces out-of-body experiences and trance work. Historically, they've used knowledge gained from communicating with the spirit world or another realm to help heal the sick and escort deceased souls safely to the afterlife. According to Curott, "It's kind of remarkable when you enter this realm and find that the things you do can actually effect change. You come back from the realm of the spirit with the gift of healing with wisdom, and realize that the world you're living in is sacred."

SOLITARY

If you're not a people person, a solo practice may be for you. There's no need to belong to a coven, and you can have it your way. That's what appealed to Maryland florist Heather Brooks. "I follow my own path—there is no right or wrong path," she says. "You don't have to deal with the politics that sometimes invade covens and can ultimately destroy them." Solo practitioners are often eclectic, but can follow any tradition.

TECH WITCH

The internet has allowed witches to connect around the world. Now it's possible to join a coven thousands of miles from home. These witches view computers as the modern equivalent of a cauldron. "Most electronics, like cell phones, laptops and tablets, have quartz crystals inside them. Quartz is piezoelectric, which means it generates voltage on its surface when compressed or bent," says Lily Johnson, a tech witch from Alexandria, Virginia. "Emojis can also be the evolution of sigil spells— which are visual forms of emotional energy with an intention. Those little pictures can still be understood by people who speak different languages." No surprise, these gadget-savvy witches embrace apps for tracking weather and lunar cycles.

TRADITIONAL

Traditional witches, also known as folk witches, strive to honor the Old Craft ceremonies and rituals of their ancestors, predating the birth of Wicca. British traditional witch Michael Howard has described it as "any non-Gardnerian, non-Alexandrian, non-Wiccan or premodern form of the craft." Three of the most common forms of traditional include Feri Tradition (strong emphasis on sexual mysticism), Cochrane's Craft (veneration of the horned god and

The internet has allowed witches from around the world to connect, learn and practice together.

Sea and water witches often conduct their magical work by the water, and rituals may involve swimming, bathing or collecting shells or sand.

I'M INTERESTED IN THE BALANCE OF NATURE, BUT I DON'T DO WICCA. I'M MORE OF A [GENERAL] PAGAN; IT'S VERY RELAXING.

Heather Brooks

mother goddess as well as their children) and Sabbatic craft (a mix of sorcery magic and Christianity).

WICCA

The United States officially recognized Wicca as a religion in 1986, and it's currently one of the fastest growing faiths in America. Gerald Gardner is often credited with establishing modern Wicca in England in the 1950s. Wiccans practice assorted forms of witchcraft, and worship nature and Earth cycles. "The general belief system is really not all that different from any other religion in that it encourages the threefold law—do what thou wilt and harm none, which is the same as the Christian golden rule," explains Sandi Liss, a longtime Wiccan and owner of metaphysical bookstore SoulJourney in Butler, New Jersey. "However, we honor the goddess and her consort, a horned god, and the changes of the seasons and the moon phases." There are myriad sects of Wicca including Gardnerian, which is the most direct lineage to Gardner's practice and requires an oath-based initiation into a coven; Alexandrian, founded by Alex Sanders, is similar but brings in additional gods. Both focus on gender polarity and celebrate the relationship between the goddess and god and believe that only a witch can make another witch. There are three levels to the initiation process, known as first, second and third degrees. A third degree gets the title of high priestess or priest. Seax-Wica is similar but does away with much of the hierarchical structure, while forms like Norse, Celtic and Druid bring in deities from other traditions. —*Amy L. Hogan*

Creativity & the *Craft*

Modern witches are manifesting their magic through the arts.

For me, there is nothing more magical than writing something; I start with a blank slate—a tabula rasa—and turn nothing into something unique. I *create*.

I write about this *wordcraft*, or word witchcraft, in my book, *The Magical Writing Grimoire*. I explain a poem can be a spell for manifestation or release of toxicity, just as using a colored ink in a journal can beautify while also symbolizing intent or conjuring a feeling. Harnessing your creativity means using your most potent, unique energy. There is nothing more powerful than that.

Consider the incantation *Abracadabra*. Yes, it may have become a silly phrase in movies about kid wizards, but its ancient origins reveal a deeper meaning. It's thought to have come from Hebrew or Aramaic, meaning, "I will create as I speak" or "I create like the word." It was a magical formula used to conjure beneficial spirits and protect one's health, and it was written on sacred stones.

The fact that a word meaning "create" is so closely associated with magic reveals the inherent connection. To make is to be magical. To create is to conjure. To express oneself is a way of tapping into the very essence of the witch—an individual, a rebel, a dreamer, a thinker, someone beating their own drum.

MAGICAL USE OF ENERGY

"There is a lot of intersection between creativity and witchcraft," says Courtney Leigh Jameson, creator of Crimson Sage Apothecary. "For instance, ritual in itself is not only a mode of creative expression, but also a way to garner inspiration. I utilize the act of ritual in order to attain both, but at different times."

So how does witchery inspire what Jameson crafts for her shop? "When

❀ Botanical candles (like this floral version from Marvel + Moon) can help inspire your inner artist.

it comes to things I make by hand, I consider it energy workings," Jameson explains. "It actually helps me to create conduits of energy with certain intentions because I personally like to physically create things in order to represent that which I want to manifest in my life, or in someone else's life if I'm making something for them."

For Trista Edwards, a poet and creator of Marvel + Moon botanical candles, the written word is also intimately tied up in her magic. "I don't know if witchcraft led me to poetry or if poetry led me to witchcraft. To me, they are one and the same."

Edwards describes being a young girl performing rituals and writing her own spells and incantations: "The motivation back then was to be creative and make the mundane magical."

Just as words shift energy, they also inspire her candle-making. "The candle is a very important tool for me to magically shift energy and generate creativity. It's a vessel to hold symbols, and it exists as a ritualistic object. To me, magic, witchcraft, poetry and candles are all vessels of action and bearers of symbol."

Music is another space where witches also enchant. Artists like Lana Del Rey, FKA twigs, Sevdaliza, Chelsea Wolfe and Dia Luna all embrace the otherworldly in their songs.

Singer-songwriter Anne Deming, whose 2020 album *Spells & Stories* was inspired after a trip to the Middle East left her feeling "literally bewitched," likens the process of making music to cooking. "You mix sounds, words, phrases and instruments together to create," she says. "The result is a type of magic."

❧ Ritual kits and altar decor (like this box from Crimson Sage Apothecary) can readily be found online.

> **"WHEN YOU THINK OF THE BASIS OF MAGIC, IT'S ABOUT CREATING SOMETHING THAT WASN'T THERE BEFORE. SOMEONE WHO HAS THE CAPACITY TO CREATE A SONG OR A PAINTING HAS TO BE OPEN TO THAT."**
>
> *Astrologer Adama Sesay*

TRANSFORMATIONS LARGE AND SMALL

Graphic artist and illustrator Lisa Sterle found inspiration in her own history for her Modern Witch Tarot deck. "I remember making a little book of shadows when I was like 12, and conspiring to find a way to sneak out of the house during a full moon so I could begin my new life as a witch," Sterle told Liminal11.com. "The idea that there's this wealth of power within you, that you just need to trust yourself to tap into, is an inspiring thought."

With swoon-worthy illustrations of diverse people, Sterle's contemporary take on the traditional Waite-Smith tarot deck has no doubt helped people feel more seen in a landscape where the canon of magical texts seemed (and sometimes still is) overwhelmingly white and male—or culturally appropriated from practitioners the world over. "I wanted to make something that young women of all kinds could see themselves reflected in and feel understood," says Sterle.

And the cards even serve as a way for her to further her own creativity. "I pull out my deck and do a reading whenever I'm feeling particularly stressed out, creatively blocked or indecisive, and it helps so much to be able to frame my feelings and put them into words."

Creativity can also physically transform us. The poet, artist and DJ Juliana Huxtable—who describes herself as a "cyborg, cu*t, priestess, witch, Nuwaubian princess"—uses

MODERN WITCH TAROT DECK

metallic paint and mixed media to transform her body in self-portraits, which make compelling statements about identity and power.

But how you play with creativity and magic is entirely up to you—and it can be found in the everyday and the

STUMPED? TURN TO THE STARS

As an astrologist, Adama Sesay, founder of Lilith Astrology (lilithastrology.com), frequently sees people who say they are stuck creatively and are looking to find answers in the cosmos.

"During a reading, we look toward past-life traumas and energy blocking that might be holding you back," explains Sesay, a self-described "modern witch." "Then holistically we look at your current challenges and figure out the steps you can take to get past the block and manifest yourself."

Often, the block is resolved by learning to be open, so one can be in the headspace to forge something new. "The first part of magic is in your mind," she says. "In the community we have tools—rituals, our deities, etc.—but if I'm not willing to open up my mind, I'm just wearing crystals and staring at the stars."

"WITCHES ARE THE ORIGINAL ACTIVISTS.... I NEVER WANT TO BE TOO FLUFFY AND LOVE AND LIGHT AND GLITTER AND UNICORNS AND WE'RE ALL GONNA DO YOGA. YES, I'M F*ING STYLISH AND I LOVE BEAUTY, BUT DON'T DISCREDIT THE FACT THAT I'M AN ACTUAL PRACTICING WITCH."**

❧ *Artist-activist Bri Luna*

mundane. Artist and activist Bri Luna—who created the hugely popular The Hoodwitch website (thehoodwitch.com) to provide "everyday magic for the modern mystic"—has said she uses makeup

✻ "Lil' Marvel" by poet and artist Juliana Huxtable appears on *Kiss My Genders'* cover (artbook.com).

as a form of ritual. "It's such a deeply personal experience where I listen to music that will inspire my look.... I truly just love the transformative powers of it; you can literally become anything that you want to be. There is no limit to your imagination and to the many looks that you can conjure up with makeup and practice."

Luna also recently cocurated an art show *Goodwitch/Badwitch* exploring "the intersection of contemporary art, ritual and witchcraft/Brujería."

BRINGING THE COMMUNITY TOGETHER

More and more people are exploring witchcraft and speaking out about their own personal ways of making magic, and this is inspiring conversations around acceptance and inclusivity in the craft. We want witch communities that make space for all sorts of beliefs and approaches. We want magical tools and magazines and spaces that reflect our beautiful diversity and multilayered backgrounds.

On my @Ritual_Poetica Instagram account, I share poems, designs and stories—all in an effort to show other magic-makers that we shouldn't mindlessly follow a Witchcraft 101 book and pursue just one path or practice. Most of what I share are ponderings and practices that can help people find healing and creativity and autonomy.

And I'm not alone. Modern witches are taking to Instagram to share art and quotes about their own witchy ways. For example, Gaby Herstik, author of *Inner Witch*, runs an account dedicated

✻ Anne Deming casts a spell with songs like "Haunted" (annedeming.com).

to shadowy, sacred oracle collages— showcasing images of herself—that she creates. It feels powerful and magical just looking at them.

There is an abundance of witchy creators making things to better others' lives. People are also creating their own witchy zines—I recently enjoyed *Small Spells Healing & Self-Help* by Rachel Howe, a captivating collection of essays

EXERCISES TO GET CREATIVE

- Paint images of your homeland(s) as a way of communicating and connecting with your ancestors.

- Write a poem that manifests something you want that you can speak aloud as an incantation.

- Decorate a space in your home utilizing colors and items that tap into nature's elements.

- Hold a photo shoot for yourself; dress as a witch or magical archetype who inspires you.

- Create a dance to conjure your inner magical power; as you move, feel yourself revving up your energy.

- Create your own zine of spells and rituals; make copies and hand it out to friends.

- Do your makeup with intention; let each color you use symbolize a feeling or goal.

and illustrations. And Etsy shops like LunaLumi offer handmade goods (T-shirts, tarot decks, candleholders, charm necklaces) for new witches who are looking to connect with specific items that strike a chord.

The witch is the natural "other." Throughout time she has been misunderstood, vilified, reduced, erased and often marginalized. Perhaps that is why the witchcraft community is making space for creativity in all of its many forms—because self-expression helps to reflect the uniquely individual ways we exist in this world; because we all have something to offer, no matter what our background may be; and because we can all learn from one another's poems, songs, handmade crafts or paintings. —*Lisa Marie Basile*

A BOOK OF SHADOWS AND ELEMENTS OF NATURE

A to Z

*From amulets to zodiac signs, everything
a good witch (or a bad one!) should know.*

AN AMULET PENDANT

AMULETS

Amulets possess an intrinsic power that provides protection for the wearer from evil deeds or dark magic. They are thought to absorb negative energy and bring good luck. As their power increases when worn close to the body, amulets are often a pendant, ring or bracelet, but they may be sewn into hidden pockets in clothing. Usually fashioned from precious metals, crystals or gemstones, they may also be made of materials such as wood or even animal bones.

BOOK OF SHADOWS

Like Wikipedia for witchcraft, a book of shadows is essentially a repository of traditions and rules of a coven, including knowledge about spell work and magic. Gerald Gardner, one of the first prominent Wicca practitioners, created one for his coven in the 1940s, and many others continued to followed its blueprint over the ensuing decades. These books, which can also exist in a digital format, are held in secret, usually by the high priest or priestess of the coven. These days, individual witches will also keep their own personal book of shadows, recording spells, incantations and herb lore, as well as reflections on their own practice.

CONE OF POWER

When witches gather in a circle to perform a magic ritual, they will draw upon their own psychic energy to power it. Performing ritual acts such as dancing, chanting or drumming raises the energy from their bodies and it forms into a cone shape, with the base aligned with the consecrated circle and the point above the group. This positive energy is then directed toward the magical intent of the spell.

DUALISM

Wicca is based around a belief in the union between two opposite yet complementary deities: a goddess (female) and a god (male). This duality is reflected in the Wiccan view of nature and the world, in characteristics such as light/dark and intuition/logic. Balance and harmony in the world around us and within the practitioners are important. This need not occur at the same time; some Wiccans have a very goddess-centered practice in order to balance the predominance of centuries of worship of male deities.

ELDER

A member of the honeysuckle family, the elder tree is a sacred tree associated with witchcraft. It is often called the "witch's tree" because nearly all of its parts—bark, leaves, berries—are used for healing, as well as in the production of protection spells. The wood is also used for the making of magic wands, and in Ireland, witches were said to fly riding on elder branches. In some lore, witches can transform into an elder tree.

FAMILIARS

The black cat is the most widely known familiar, but these supernatural assistants come in a variety of forms. They are usually animals, especially small creatures, including dogs, ferrets, mice, rabbits or toads, although they can be humanlike in form as well. Familiars assist witches in their spell work, act as protectors, and legend has it that they've even used their ability to shape-shift so they can serve as spies in gathering information.

A FAMILIAR IN THE FORM OF A BLACK CAT

143

"WITCHES' SABBATH"
BY FRANCISCO GOYA

ROMAN STATUE OF HECATE

GOYA

Witches feature prominently in many of the paintings of famed 18th-century Spanish artist Francisco Goya, most notably a series of six paintings purchased by the Duke and Duchess of Osuna. In "Witches' Sabbath," Satan appears as a goat amid a coven of semi-clad witches interspersed with babies, both alive and dead. This is a reference to the Basque witch trials of 1610, where women were accused of witchcraft and of sacrificing their children. Rather than a warning about witches, Goya's paintings were actually his protest against how the church had led Spanish society into a mire of superstition and ignorance.

HECATE

The goddess of witches, Hecate is the daughter of Greek titans Perses and Asteria and is associated with the moon, witchcraft, herbalism and the creatures of the night. Her realm is beyond the world of the living; she guards the boundaries between worlds and is also the goddess of ghosts and restless spirits. Often depicted with three faces—representing the realms of the heavens, Earth and underworld—modern lore most commonly calls her the Crone Goddess. Shakespeare mentions her in both *A Midsummer Night's Dream* and *Macbeth*.

IMP

Imps are small, mischievous demons who, according to legend, serve as familiars for witches, assisting them in their work. They are generally depicted as being quite ugly, with large ears and horns and leathery batlike wings, and are known for having a penchant for setting fires. Witch hunters would often charge that witches fed imps with their own blood—from their finger, breast or any skin protuberance, including warts. Carvings of imps can be found adorning medieval buildings, including cathedrals such as Lincoln Cathedral in Lincoln, England.

JINX

A jinx is a spell cast with the intention of bringing bad luck to a person. It is usually temporary and designed to cause only minor misfortune. By comparison, a hex is more powerful and lasts longer, though it is generally broken when the subject learns his or her lesson. Curses

KITCHEN WITCH DOLL

are the most serious of the negative spells and are often designed to cause grave harm that may last a lifetime. Curses may also be attached to objects, so they can afflict others beyond the initial target by mistake.

KITCHEN WITCH DOLL

Originating in Scandinavia, this poppet is made to resemble an old crone. It is displayed in the kitchen to bring good—like preventing roasts from burning—and keep evil spirits at bay.

145

OWLS

LILITH

A fierce feminine and feminist figure, Lilith has been viewed as both demon and goddess through history. Many modern Wiccan and neo-pagan practitioners, as well as secular feminists, believe her negative image is a result of a patriarchal fear of women's power. Today, Lilith represents female independence and sexuality; she is portrayed as a protector of witches.

MAY NIGHT

The night of May 1 is celebrated as Beltane, which marks the beginning of summer. There is a long tradition of festivities and rituals at this time of year to ensure a good season for crops and livestock. It is a celebration of fertility, and of the god and goddess uniting. Fire is an important component of Beltane, symbolizing purification and rebirth. Leaping over a Beltane bonfire is said to bring good fortune and fertility—both literal and metaphorical—in the form of productive and creative energy.

NECROMANCER

Necromancy is the practice of magic to summon and communicate with the dead. The living may want information from a specific departed person, or a spirit may be summoned to obtain information from other realms and even across time. The most well-known form of this involves a seance, where a practitioner who is psychically sensitive will contact the spirits, often speaking with them through a spirit board (think a Ouija board). Darker magic has also been used in order to raise the dead in corporeal form.

OWLS

While their most recent mystical association is delivering letters and messages for students at a certain School of Witchcraft and

QUEEN ANNE BOLEYN

Wizardry, owls have a long association with witches and magic. These nighttime predators are reputed to be wise, often seeing or knowing things humans cannot. The Greeks and Romans believed witches could turn into owls. Some cultures see them as a harbinger of death, or as the creature who will guide a soul to the afterlife. If you find them living in a house, you can be sure that it's haunted.

PAGAN

Paganism is a broad term that covers a range of beliefs and practices that exist outside of the major world religions. Pagan religions, known today as Neopaganism, often encompass a number of deities. Some believe that all living beings contain a spiritual essence. Many pagan religions, both old and modern, involve magic and spell work. Wicca, sometimes called pagan witchcraft, is a modern pagan religion which encompasses a variety of traditions. Other pagan religions inclue Druidry and Asatru.

QUEEN ANNE BOLEYN

Anne Boleyn was the second wife of the much-married King Henry the VIII of England. When she failed to provide him with a male heir, Henry had Anne charged with adultery, incest and treason and declared she had used magic to trick him into marriage. She was never formally charged with witchcraft, but many accused her and claimed she had features that identified her as a witch, including a sixth finger, a protruding tooth and a mole on her chin. She was beheaded in 1536.

147

RABBITS

Rabbits are often seen as the familiars of witches and, in some traditions, witches could transform into the creatures in order to travel in secret. Rabbits are associated with the moon and lunar magic. Because they live underground and are often seen entering their burrows at twilight, they are thought to be able to move between our world and other realms. Rabbit blood and bones are also used in some rituals. A rabbit's foot is a lucky charm (but not for the rabbit!).

SKIN-WALKERS

In Navajo culture, *yee naaldlooshii* or skin-walkers are a type of witch who can transform themselves into animals. In human form they may wear the pelt or antlers of their chosen creatures—hence the name skin-walker. Transformations occur at night, and the skin-walker can also control other animals.

TAROT

The tarot is a deck of cards used for divination. It consists of 78 cards of two types: the major arcana (greater secrets) and the minor arcana (lesser secrets). The suits are wands, swords, cups and circles or pentacles. The cards are used to gain insight about a person's life and provide guidance. Tarot readings are often done by people who are psychically sensitive.

UMBANDA

Umbanda is a religion of Brazil that combines beliefs brought to the country by enslaved people from Africa along with Catholicism and Indigenous beliefs. While it worships a single god, intermediary deities called Orixás and

RABBIT

TAROT DECK

A UMBANDA PRIEST

ZODIAC CHART

incantations, rituals and myths and legends from many cultures.

XORGUINA

This group of witches lived in caves throughout the mountains of the Basque region. They worshipped Mari, a goddess of the Earth and the elements. The Xorguina were the subject of the most extensive, and thankfully the last, witch hunt of the Spanish Inquisition.

YULE

Yule or Midwinter is a seasonal observation that is part of the Wheel of the Year and followed by many pagans. It celebrates the winter solstice, which occurs on Dec. 21 and marks the beginning of longer days—and that spring is on its way. Traditionally logs are burned, branches of evergreen trees are brought into the home, and gifts are exchanged—all traditions incorporated into the Christian holiday of Christmas.

spirits feature prominently. Temples are led by a psychic priest or priestess who interacts with the spirits.

LA VOLTA

La Volta, also known as the "witch's dance," is a couple's dance involving much lifting and twirling. Popular at the time of Elizabeth I, it was widely condemned because of its overtly sexual nature. Some claim the dance had been brought to France from Italy by witches, and it was so complex it must have had an origin beyond our world.

WITCHES' ALMANAC

The Witches' Almanac, first published by Elizabeth Pepper in 1971, documents information and knowledge useful to witches such as the annual lunar calendar, as well as herb lore,

ZODIAC SIGNS

Zodiac or astrological signs are based on the time and location of a person's birth, which are influenced by the position of the sun, moon and planets at that time, due to the connectedness of all things. A person's zodiac sign is based on the constellation the sun was traveling through when they were born. Each sign is associated with certain dominant personality attributes.

JULES WILKINSON *is a queer writer and comedian who lives on Wurundjeri Country in Australia. She loves writing about all things pop culture, science and food.*

CHAPTER 4

WITCHES IN POP CULTURE

*DISCOVER THE LONG HISTORY OF HAGS AND
ENCHANTRESSES IN LEGENDS AND LORE, AND FIND OUT
HOW* THE WIZARD OF OZ *FOREVER CHANGED
THE PERCEPTION OF THE WITCH. THEN CHECK OUT OTHER
POPULAR SPELL-CASTERS, FROM* SABRINA THE TEENAGE
WITCH *TO THE TRIO OF BADDIES IN* HOCUS POCUS.

BABA YAGA

The Stuff of *Fairy Tales* and *Legends*

*From Baba Yaga to Morgan le Fay,
every culture has its stories of witchy women
living in the woods.*

CIRCE

YAMA-UBA

Witches have been appearing in stories since people began telling stories. Tales told to children to teach a moral, or whispered at bedtime to scare them into behaving. Stories exchanged between adults late at night for a chill. These characters are not always named as witches; they are also called sorceresses or fairies, or maybe they are just women who have a way with herbs. Some are empirically evil, others just like to cause mischief—and occasionally they are there to save the day. But more often than not, they're more complex creatures than they originally seem.

INDEPENDENT WOMEN

Tales of mysterious women living alone and without the traditional trappings of a husband or children feature prominently in many cultures. One fascinating creation is Baba Yaga, a witch of Russian folklore who lives in the woods in a house standing on chicken legs. With her iron teeth and long, crooked nose, she embodies the stereotype of the hag, and she does occasionally eat a child or two. But she also sometimes helps those people who wander her way. In the tale of "Vasilisa the Beautiful," for instance, Baba Yaga liberates the young heroine from her abusive stepfamily…by burning their home with them inside. "Unlike the traditional godmother figure, Baba is outside the bounds of morality, and her aid often comes in menacing forms," journalist Marissa Clifford explains on vice.com.

Yama-Uba is a similarly multifaceted character in Japanese folktales. A mountain witch with unkempt hair and a filthy kimono, she lures people into her hut and eats them. Yet other stories show her as a kind being, such as the tale where she raises an orphan who goes on to become the famous hero Sakata no Kintoki.

One of the oldest recorded stories about a witch is the epic poem "The Odyssey," written by Homer in ancient Greece. The daughter of the god Helios, Circe is skilled in herbs and is often referred to as a witch-goddess. With her glorious singing, she lures sailors to her island of Aeaea, invites them to dinner, then turns them into animals. The epic's hero, Odysseus, and his men make a stop there after the Trojan War. Circe treats them to a lavish feast, where the crew eats food laced with a magical potion that turns them into pigs. The god Hermes helps Odysseus avoid Circe's spell, and she eventually takes Odysseus as a lover and turns his crew back into men.

It might sound counterintuitive, but "Renaissance scholars reasoned, it is possible that [Circe] did them a favor, as the existence of a pig, carefree and lacking in self-awareness, was preferable to the painful human existence," author Hannah Roberts writes in *iNews*. "And more recent retakes on Greek mythology have suggested Circe had good reason to react as she did, given the rampant misogyny of most men of her time." The ancient witch-goddess got a subversive update as the heroine in Madeline Miller's 2018 novel *Circe*.

MORGAN LE FAY

KATHERINE LANGFORD AS NIMUË ON *CURSED*

Likewise, powerful sorceress Morgana can be found in almost every telling of the Arthurian legend. First appearing in the 12th-century story "The Life of Merlin" by Geoffrey of Monmouth, Morgana—also known as Morgan le Fay—rules the island of Avalon. When Arthur is brought there after being wounded in battle, she heals him.

Over time, as the Arthurian stories were told and retold, Morgana went from a benevolent healer to a formidable foe. In Sir Thomas Malory's *Le Morte d'Arthur*, Morgana plots to steal Arthur's throne and indirectly causes his death. She also conspires against Guinevere, as this version presents them as romantic rivals for Lancelot. Why the change? "In the late medieval period, magic increasingly became associated with witchcraft and the devil," Marta Cobb, PhD, a medieval-English literature scholar, writes in theconversation.com. But, Cobb notes, Arthur's buddy Merlin—a male wizard—is still regarded in a kind light. "Meanwhile, Morgana is condemned for being a woman who seeks magical and political power for herself."

Morgana as the villain still persists today, in depictions like the 2019 film *The Kid Who Would Be King*. But she gets a fairer shake in Marion Zimmer Bradley's *The Mists of Avalon*, where she is a defender of the old pagan religion against the encroachment of Christianity. She and fellow Arthurian witch Nimuë, aka the Lady of the Lake, again get a modern feminist update in Netflix's 2020 hit series *Cursed*.

Witch hysteria was in full force in Renaissance Europe as William Shakespeare was writing, which may explain why witches factor into many of his plays, most famously the trio of seers in *Macbeth*. Though their role is relatively minor, the three crones drive much of the tragedy's action. After they prophesize he will be king, ruthless and ambitious Macbeth starts on a path of regicide. Further prophecies from the witches, which are deliberately worded to trick Macbeth, eventually lead to his demise.

The image of these three biddies mixing "eye of newt, toe of frog" and other nasty ingredients into their cauldron while chanting, "Double, double toil and trouble; fire, burn; and, cauldron, bubble!" has persisted for centuries.

"THE LITTLE MERMAID"

NURSERY RHYMES FROM OLDEN TIMES

Not long after Shakespeare, one of the first collections of the fairy tales we're most familiar with was published by Italian writer Giambattista Basile. *The Pentamerone* includes versions of stories such as "Cinderella" and "The Snow Queen" (the basis for *Frozen*). While the witches here are often nefarious, it's worth noting in this early form of "Rapunzel," the long-haired heroine (then called Petrosinella) learns magical arts herself and uses them to escape with her prince.

Fairy tales as a cultural phenomenon really took off in France later in the 17th century, when Charles Perrault published his collection *The Tales of Mother Goose*. Perrault's version of "The Sleeping Beauty" is an example of a story with a long and multicultural history that can be traced back to the Nordic story "*Saga of the Völsungs,*" in which Brynhild is cursed to sleep by a poisoned thorn after she angers the god Odin, and is only awakened when a man comes to her who knows no fear.

In Perrault's version, seven fairies are invited to celebrate the birth of a princess. An old fairy is angered at being overlooked (to be fair, everyone thought her dead), and curses the child to die after she pricks her finger on the spindle of a spinning wheel. One of the other fairies manages to weaken the spell so the princess will only sleep for 100 years. The inevitable happens, but the princess is awakened by a kiss from a prince.

Many have speculated that in her pointy peasant hat, Mother Goose herself is a witch, and fairy-tale collections of the late 19th and early 20th centuries often feature covers of her flying on her broom, sometimes with a cat.

MACBETH

"BY TURNS DANGEROUS AND KIND, HIDEOUS AND BEAUTIFUL, OUTCAST AND SOCIAL, [THE GRIMMS' WITCHES] ARE OFTEN...A REMINDER THAT FAIRY TALES ARE NEVER AS SIMPLE AS THEY FIRST SEEM."

— *Folklorists Sara Cleto, PhD & Brittany Warman, PhD*

In the 19th century, brothers Jacob and Wilhelm Grimm published German folklore, including a version of "The Sleeping Beauty" called "Little Briar Rose." The brothers changed the evil mothers in many stories to stepmothers and removed any sexual references, but they didn't water down the gruesomeness. In their "Hansel and Gretel," a young brother and sister are abandoned in the woods by their stepmother, where they stumble upon a house made of gingerbread and candy. Inside lives a witch who feasts on children after they've been fattened up by nibbling on her home.

That cannibalism aside, folklorists Sara Cleto, PhD, and Brittany Warman, PhD, write, "The witches of the Grimms' fairy tales occupy a far more diverse set of roles than is frequently assumed." Witches do have a positive role in some lesser-known stories. A witch takes care of a young princess exiled by her father in "The

THE MISTS OF AVALON

MARION ZIMMER BRADLEY

Goose Girl at the Well." In "The Three Spinners," three deformed witches help a lazy girl forced to spin yarn in order to marry a prince. At the wedding, they say their deformities were caused by too much spinning, and the prince declares his wife will never have to spin again.

Danish author Hans Christian Andersen wrote his fairy tales featuring witches. In "The Little Mermaid," a witch gives a young mermaid what she wants—transformation into a human girl and a chance to be with the man she loves—but she cuts out the mermaid's tongue for payment, and tells her walking on land will feel like walking on knives.

Through the years these stories of powerful witchy women have persisted, changed and of course been Disneyfied, but they will no doubt continue to endure.

—*Jules Wilkinson*

The Salem witch trials have been a popular subject for authors and filmmakers.

Literary Spell-Caster

In Hour of the Witch, *author Chris Bohjalian weaves a thriller of a tale rooted in 1662 Boston.*

New York Times bestselling author Chris Bohjalian has long been fascinated with complex female protagonists. (His popular 2018 novel, *The Flight Attendant*, was turned into a series on HBO Max in 2020.) And in his newest historical suspense novel, *Hour of the Witch*—which is set in Massachusetts on the eve of the Salem trials—the main character, Mary Deerfield, embodies a strong female to the letter.

We sat down with the Vermont-based author to discover what inspired him to do a deep dive into our nation's complicated Puritan history, what he hopes readers come to understand about life in the Massachusetts Bay Colony in the 1600s and, ultimately, what it is about witches that fascinates him the most.

How much research did you do before you began writing *Hour of the Witch*?
It probably took about a year and a half of researching witchcraft, reacquainting myself with Puritan

theology, learning about Puritan law and learning about divorce.

I also studied what it was like to live in Boston in 1662. Next, I focused on the whole aura of Satan's predestination, justification and sanctification in Puritan culture. For the men and women of the Massachusetts Bay Colony, Satan was real. Satan was every bit as sentient a being in their world as their lord and savior Jesus Christ. Witches and witchcraft were real fears.

It's fascinating the way you focused *Hour of the Witch* entirely on Mary's story.
Mary is in every single scene in the book and every single scene is from her perspective. I viewed this as Mary's story

Public shaming figured strongly in the Puritan hunt for witches.

and what it was like for her to be married to Thomas, who demeans her. He says she has a brain that's made of cheese and also, because she's a woman, going back to Eve, he thinks there's something duplicitous about her. On the one hand, she's not smart; on the other hand, she's too smart for her own good. The book is a bit of a mystery and I wanted the reader to only be able to know what Mary knows. You don't know who planted the devil's tines in the yard and why. You don't know what kind of malfeasance someone is up to. We just know it isn't Mary and that Mary is being wrongly accused.

fork was considered the devil's tines. In fact, it wasn't until the late 17th century that parts of Europe started using forks. When I came across the obscure fact that John Winthrop, one of the Massachusetts Bay Colony leaders, almost caused a scandal because he had a fork in the house with three tines, the devil's tines, I thought that was so interesting and that's one of the places where the book began.

Why are we as a culture so fascinated with witches?

Historically, strong women and smart women have often been a threat to men, and historically, the women accused of being witches were, at the very least, opinionated. Certainly that was true in 17th-century America. One of the most notorious Boston women hanged as a witch was the governor's sister-in-law. Why was she hanged? It went back to a few years earlier, when she had the audacity to call out the carpenters who were building her house for their shoddy work.

There were other examples of witch trials that historians find fascinating. Can you share which events affected you the most when writing the book?

Whenever we think of [American] witch trials, we think of 1692 and the 20 men and women hanged that year, but in 1662 there was a huge witch outbreak in Hartford and six women were hanged. That didn't get the same play—I don't know why, especially because six women in 1662 was a lot of people to be hanged. In Boston and Salem there was a fear

Without giving away any plot points, the lowly fork ultimately plays a huge role in the book.
The Puritans didn't use forks. They only used a knife and spoon because the

that Satan was in their midst. In 1662, there hadn't been a hanging in Boston in six years. Then the hanging happened in Hartford and Boston was worried, which is why I set *Hour of the Witch* in 1662.

So witches were largely considered a threat to male-dominated culture?

It was a way to keep women down whenever men felt threatened and to keep women in their place. Also, the women who were hanged or accused of witchcraft had arcane knowledge that men didn't have, whether it was in the healing arts or

Rebecca Nurse, chained after her conviction for witchcraft in June 1692; she was hanged one month later.

midwifery. One of the most prominent women exiled from the Colony was Anne Hutchinson, who was a midwife.

Who are some of your favorite witches in literature?

The Scarlet Letter is a great novel but I was far more interested in *The Crucible*, since it builds to a witch trial and I love courtroom dramas.

How else have you touched on the witches in your work?

Among the books I'm probably known best for is *Midwives*, a novel about a midwife on trial for manslaughter after a home birth goes tragically wrong, set in 1981 in Vermont. I always viewed it as a rather *Crucible*-like novel. It's essentially a witch hunt where the midwives of New England of the early 1980s are the witches being hunted by a very male medical establishment that feels threatened.

Your book is pretty well timed to the world we're living in now.

When one of the magistrates calls Mary "a nasty woman," the reference will not be lost on my readers. And I think it's a great time for this book because it's escapism. In 1662, they didn't know about viruses and were grinding up toads and blowing them up a nostril with a piece of straw. I love Mary. She's smart, she's courageous and, like many of my heroines, she's deeply human. She's a powerful woman and she's imperfect. She's real.

Do you agree that there's a different take on witches today?

Here's what I think is great: We have come to love witches because we've all

A strong male establishment questioning an independent-thinking female isn't new in Bohjalian's work.

begun to understand that whether it's a belief system or a different view of the world, witches aren't satanic, they aren't evil. Witches historically have either been the smartest women in the world and thus the most threatening, or they have simply been women with skill sets that other people didn't appreciate. I also believe that we no longer think of witches as older women who live alone and have big warts on their noses or the

other weird male stereotype of witches as hot women dancing naked around a bonfire. We've transcended that. We understand that the people we called witches were actually the independent thinkers, the iconoclasts, the people who simply didn't toe the party line.

LAMBETH HOCHWALD *is a New York City-based writer who focuses on trends, health and issues of importance to women.*

More *Great Lit* Witches

Ask literary buffs and they'll tell you that witches are some of the most intriguing of characters to grace the pages. Sometimes sinister, sometimes simply misunderstood—here, eight of the most famous.

▼ MORGAN LE FAY

There have been scores of incarnations of this mysterious sorceress from the Arthurian legend, who first appeared in medieval poet Geoffrey of Monmouth's "The Life of Merlin." In some tales, notably *Le Morte d'Arthur* by Sir Thomas Malory in 1469 and T.H. White's *Once and Future King* series from the 1930s, she's a malevolent force challenging her half brother King Arthur. Other times she's more of a complex healer. Mary Zimmer Bradley flipped the story and made her the star in 1983's *Mists of Avalon*, where Morgan is the defender of old pagan religions.

▲ HERMIONE GRANGER

Fans of the massively popular *Harry Potter* series often say that Harry wouldn't have survived the first book if it weren't for his muggle-born pal Hermione (played by Emma Watson). Despite not discovering her powers until age 11, Hermione is the "brightest witch of her age," and fastidious about her studies. Still, Hermione knows: "Books! And cleverness! There are more important things!—Friendship! And bravery!"

▲ THE GRAND HIGH WITCH

In Roald Dahl's imagination, witches don't look anything like the stereotypical witch who wears a pointy hat and rides atop a broomstick. In *The Witches*, published in 1983, the witches' main goal in life is to transform children into mice. This imaginative book has led to many a film adaptation, including a 1990 film starring Anjelica Huston and a 2020 film directed by Robert Zemeckis starring Anne Hathaway (above).

◄ THE WICKED WITCH OF THE WEST

In his 1900 novel, *The Wonderful Wizard of Oz*, L. Frank Baum introduced the world to the baddest of the bad—The Wicked Witch of the West, who is the ultimate (blue) monkey wrench in the plans of the Good Witch of the North and Dorothy Gale of Kansas. But there are two sides to every story, and Gregory Maguire gave the WWW—now named Elphaba—her due in his 1995 novel *Wicked*, reframing her as a savior for animal rights.

▼ THE WITCHES OF EASTWICK

A group of three women with day jobs—Jane (a cellist who floats on air), Sukie (a writer who can turn milk into cream) and Alexandra (a sculptor who can make thunderstorms appear)—are the witches in John Updike's 1984 dark-comedy novel that was later turned into a memorable 1987 film starring Susan Sarandon, Michelle Pfeiffer and Cher.

▶ JADIS, THE WHITE WITCH

In C.S. Lewis' *The Lion, the Witch and the Wardrobe* from his *The Chronicles of Narnia* series, this icy enchantress is a major force to be reckoned with. In the 1950 novel, she has the power to put the world into a 24/7 wintry un-wonderland, and she shows her strength when leading a rebellion against her sister. Hers is a saga that's one to remember.

The Enduring Effects of the *Emerald City*

The Wizard of Oz *introduced the concept of good and bad witches and changed magic forever.*

❄ Dorothy is shocked to learn she's killed the Wicked Witch of the East with her house.

veryone is familiar with the question. Dorothy and her house are blown from Kansas to Oz by a twister and crash in Munchkinland. The young farm girl (Judy Garland) steps out into a suddenly full-color world where she is greeted by a beautiful woman (Billie Burke) who asks, "Are you a good witch or a bad witch?" Terrified, Dorothy says she's not a witch at all, that witches are old and mean and ugly, but the ballgown-clad beauty explains that's just not true, that she herself is a good witch.

The film, and the L. Frank Baum books on which it's based, have entertained generations, but they also had a profound effect on the modern mythology of witches. And the story of their creation has surprisingly feminist roots.

A WITCH OF A DIFFERENT COLOR

For centuries, Western mythology painted witches as ugly, old crones who used dark arts to bring misfortune to the innocent. Women accused of witchcraft were persecuted across medieval Europe and the New World, while 19th century, fairy tales by the Grimm Brothers exacerbated the bad publicity with evil witches like the ones in "Sleeping Beauty" and "Hansel and

❖ Margaret Hamilton as the Wicked Witch plots to get Dorothy, "and her little dog, too!"

Gretel." No wonder Dorothy gasped at the insinuation she might be a witch.

Women's rights advocate Matilda Joslyn Gage, who worked alongside suffragettes including Susan B. Anthony and Elizabeth Cady Stanton, challenged these stereotypes in her 1893 book *Woman, Church, and State*. Gage exposed how the patriarchal structure of the Christian church had been responsible for centuries of oppression of women, and claimed the persecution of witches was an extension of that. "If for 'witches,' we read 'women,'" she wrote,

"we gain a fuller understanding of the cruelties inflicted by the church upon this portion of humanity."

Gage claimed the term "witch" originally referred to a woman of "superior knowledge." She postulated magic was the "knowledge of the effect of certain natural, but generally unknown laws," and noted many things once held to be magic could be explained by science. Magic, Gage argued, was not good or evil, although its consequences could be. The good or evil lay in the motivation of the person using it.

These concepts can be found throughout the pages of Baum's 14 books about the land of Oz, and there's a good reason: Baum married Gage's daughter Maud in 1882. While Gage at first was disappointed her daughter gave up her studies to be a housewife, she eventually came around to her son-in-law and encouraged him to write down the fantastical tales he told his sons, according to Evan I. Schwartz, author of *Finding Oz: How L. Frank Baum Discovered the Great American Story.* It's pretty clear Gage had a hand in the plot development as well; in one letter to Baum, she even suggested he "maybe bring in a cyclone."

Baum finally published *The Wonderful Wizard of Oz* in 1900, after Matilda's death, but her imprint is clear. Baum's witches are often wise women and magic is not inherently evil. Baum's books have good witches alongside wicked ones, disrupting the centuries' old hegemony that his mother-in-law had railed against.

MATILDA JOSLYN GAGE

The books were critically acclaimed and huge bestsellers, with the Library of Congress declaring *The Wonderful Wizard of Oz* to be "America's greatest and best-loved homegrown fairy tale."

A FILM FOR THE AGES

It was the 1939 movie adaptation, directed by Victor Fleming, however, that truly immortalized the Emerald City. *The Wizard of Oz* is the most-watched film...ever, according to the Library of Congress. Lines like "There's no place like home" and "I don't think we're in Kansas anymore" are instantly recognizable, and generations of kids have been terrified by Margaret Hamilton's cackling green Wicked Witch of the West.

Countless critics have theories as to why the film holds up so well more than 80 years later. Certainly it's a coming-of-age story with much to say about understanding one's own abilities. At the film's close, the Cowardly Lion (Bert Lahr) learns he had courage all along; the Tin Man (Jack Haley) always had heart; the Scarecrow (Ray Bolger), smarts; and Dorothy could have gone home whenever she pleased—no wizard required. The effects were stunning at the time and still stand up today. Plus, who hasn't yearned to go over the rainbow and see the wide world beyond their own home? And of course—those wondrous witches.

"Glinda and the Witch of the West are the only two symbols of power in a film that is largely about the powerless," Salman Rushdie wrote in *The New Yorker.* "The power center of the film is a triangle at whose points are Glinda, Dorothy and the Witch; the fourth point, at which the Wizard is thought for most of the film

to stand, turns out to be an illusion. The power of men, it is suggested, is illusory; the power of women is real."

Where Baum's books hadn't linked the witches' appearances to their deeds, the movie goes there. The Wicked Witch is the classic stereotype—a hideous hag with bright-green skin. In contrast, Glinda is the sparkling embodiment of genteel feminine beauty. When Dorothy tells Glinda she has never heard of a beautiful witch before, Glinda responds with, "Only bad witches are ugly." It was an idea Burke, who played Glinda, apparently bought into. In her biography *With Powder on My Nose*, she writes, "To be a woman...means giving, understanding, bearing, and loving. To begin with, these things require being as attractive as possible." She also reportedly insisted on referring to Glinda as a fairy rather than a witch!

But Rushdie would bet on black. "Of the two witches, good and bad, can there be anyone who'd choose to spend five minutes with Glinda?" he wrote. "Of course, Glinda is 'good' and the Wicked Witch 'bad' but Glinda is a silly pain in the neck, and the Wicked Witch is lean and mean. Check out their clothes: frilly pink versus slim line black. No contest."

While many "good witches" followed in the spirit of Glinda, the Wicked Witch of the West would get her due.

FINALLY DEFYING GRAVITY

There are two sides to every story. And Gregory Maguire explored the Wicked Witch's perspective in a series of novels beginning with 1995's *Wicked.*

"I became interested in the nature of evil, and whether one really could be

ELPHABA IS...A REALLY SMART GIRL, WHO'S ALSO OUTSPOKEN AND DEFENSIVE BECAUSE SHE'S AN OUTCAST. THERE ARE FORCES TRYING TO KEEP HER DOWN, BUT SHE'S DETERMINED TO...MAKE A DIFFERENCE IN THE WORLD.

—Actress Idina Menzel

Kristin Chenoweth and Idina Menzel are a "Popular" pair in the original cast of *Wicked*.

born bad," Maguire has said. "I considered briefly writing a novel about Hitler... when I realized nobody had ever written about the second-most evil character in our collective American subconscious: the Wicked Witch of the West."

The novel is a retelling of Baum's first book, starting years before Dorothy's arrival. It follows the life of the green-skinned Elphaba—who will eventually become that most wicked of witches. When she attends Shiz University, Elphaba rooms with one of the most popular girls in school, Glinda.

Elphaba becomes aware of the increasing oppression of the animals of Oz by the Wizard. And after the murder of her favorite professor at the Wizard's command, Elphaba becomes active in animal rights, which leads her into opposition with the Wizard and Glinda.

In 2003, the book was adapted into the Broadway musical *Wicked* starring Idina Menzel (who later voiced Elsa in *Frozen*) as Elphaba and Kristin Chenoweth as Glinda. Both actresses said they took cues from their famous film counterparts.

"One of the things that struck me is [the Wicked Witch's] cackle, which we equate with evil," Menzel, who won a Tony for the role, told *Playbill*. "I wanted the audience to hear that same cackle when she is a kid. And then you see it's just a big old roaring laugh that comes from a real place. It doesn't come from evil. But it's interpreted that way by people who want to vilify her."

Wicked remains one of the most successful musicals of all time, with productions of the show staged around the world.   *—Jules Wilkinson*

Teen Witch *Woes*

Changing from a girl to a woman is a crazy time,
even before adding spells to the mix.

⟨⟩ **The teen coven in *The Craft* still resonates with outsiders.**

Misunderstood and condemned for unusual interests: There is perhaps no more apt metaphor for being a teenage girl than the teenage witch. This might explain why coming-of-age sorceresses have been a staple in books, TV shows and movies since *Sabrina the Teen-Age Witch* first graced the pages of the Archie comics in the 1960s.

The teen witch craze really took off in earnest in 1996, when the world was introduced to the film *The Craft* and the TV show *Sabrina the Teenage Witch* mere months apart.

Brimming with 1990s fashion fads like brown lipstick and neck chokers, *The Craft* follows four high school students—Sarah (Robin Tunney), Nancy (Fairuza Balk), Rochelle (Rachel True) and Bonnie (Neve Campbell) —struggling with serious challenges

including poverty, racism and abuse. Drawn together by an interest in magic, they form an intense bond. As the girls become closer, their powers grow, and they use them to fight back. The rage of the characters and the thrill they get from finally unleashing it still resonates with audiences 25 years later. Nancy's sassy declaration, "We *are* the weirdos!" has become a rallying cry for every misunderstood teen who found strength in outsider status.

It's a common theme in the genre and in teen life, as feminist Erica Jong shared on her website. "Adolescence is a time when witchcraft exercises a great fascination. Disempowered by society and overwhelmed with physical changes, teenage girls fall in love with the idea of forming covens."

The Craft was a surprise hit when it was released, and has since become a cult

classic, especially among young women. Alas, the film is also a cautionary tale. The foursome's spells have increasingly dire consequences, the coven fractures and the friends turn on each other, falling into the trope that female relationships are toxic. Good-girl Sarah gets to keep her powers, while the others lose theirs. And poor Nancy ends up restrained and mad in an institution— seemingly a warning for young women who might fight back too hard and stray from the role society defines for her. (A 2020 update—*The Craft: Legacy*—did away with the bad-girl Nancy storyline but lost "the bewitching quality" of the first film, according to *The New York Times* and many a viewer.)

⁂ Hermione (Emma Watson) in *Harry Potter and the Chamber of Secrets.*

⁂ Half-witch, half-mortal, Sabrina the Teen-Age Witch debuted in *Archie* comics in 1962. She had her own comic book from 1971–2009.

MELISSA JOAN HART IN *SABRINA THE TEENAGE WITCH*

wacky witch aunts, Hilda and Zelda, and her magical, quipping cat, Salem. Sabrina dealt with the typical trials and tribulations of a sitcom teenager and used her magic to help her friends. As one might expect, it wasn't always smooth spell-casting, such as the time Sabrina turns the most popular girl at school into a pineapple. "The magic was a metaphor for a young girl learning to control her desires and emotions, as well as an excuse to showcase a 6-foot flan," creator Nell Scovell told *The Guardian*.

As different as *Sabrina* and *The Craft* may have been, together they helped create an association between girl power and witchcraft. "Historically, witches have been outcasts, and much of this unease clearly stems from a fear of female force," University of Warwick professor

Infinitely more frothy but no less fun, *Sabrina the Teenage Witch* came out that same year as part of ABC's teen-centered TGIF Friday night lineup. The series starred Melissa Joan Hart as Sabrina Spellman, who lives with her

Rachel Moseley, PhD, wrote in her paper "Glamorous Witchcraft." "The teenage witch genre articulates a new powerful image of femininity. It's not that the hag and herb potions have become hip; rather, witchcraft has become synonymous with power and girlie magic."

HEAD OF THE CLASS

The most beloved young witch for many readers will forever be Hermione Granger of the *Harry Potter* series. Hermione is incredibly smart, magically talented and described by those around her as "the brightest witch of her age." Her skills are repeatedly integral in saving the day—whether it's solving Snape's potion riddle or using a time-turner not only to cram in extra classes but also to save Sirius Black and the hippogriff Buckbeak.

In between battling dark forces including the Death Eaters and He Who Must Not Be Named, Hermione also finds time to start a social justice movement for oppressed house-elves (sadly, the films omit this achievement). It's no wonder Hermione has become a feminist icon, with her image often

AMBER BENSON AND ALYSON HANNIGAN IN *BUFFY THE VAMPIRE SLAYER*

❧ Sabrina (Kiernan Shipka) gets super spooky after performing a mandrake spell on *Chilling Adventures of Sabrina.*

adorning the handmade signs at women's rallies with the slogan, "What would Hermione do?"

Emma Watson, who portrayed the young witch in all eight movies, told *Entertainment Weekly* Hermione's feisty nature and willingness to speak up "gave other women permission to feel that they were allowed to take up space."

A less skilled, but adorably amusing, student is Mildred Hubble from *The Worst Witch,* based on a series of books by Jill Murphy. In a recent Netflix adaptation, the good-hearted Mildred (Bella Ramsey, better known as the wee-but-fierce Lady Lyanna Mormont from *Game of Thrones)* accidentally finds herself enrolled in Miss Cackle's Academy for Witches, where she has goofy misadventures and earns the title the "worst witch" in the school.

Mildred's efforts to master magic parallel the teenage struggle to learn how to behave as the adults they are becoming. A similar theme is explored in the 1989 Japanese animated film *Kiki's Delivery Service,* which follows a young witch as she takes her first steps toward independence. When Kiki is plagued with self-doubt, this is mirrored in the loss of her ability to fly.

❋ Ashley Nicole Williams, Jessica Sutton and Taylor Hickson are military witches in *Motherland: Fort Salem*.

WOKE AND WOMANLY

Magic can also serve as a potent symbol for a girl's discovery of her sexuality, which can be both exciting and dangerous. "[Teen] witches usually acquire their powers at a moment which both marks adolescence and captures the moment of transition from child to woman, and thus the potential attainment of adult femininity and (sexual) power," writes Moseley.

Consider the cult phenomenon *Buffy the Vampire Slayer*: Buffy's (Sarah Michelle Gellar) best friend Willow Rosenberg (Alyson Hannigan) starts to explore magic at the same time she starts developing crushes. When she meets Tara Maclay (Amber Benson) at a college Wicca group, the two fall in love while exploring the craft. With the WB network uncomfortable showing explicit intimacy between two women, creator Joss Whedon had to fight to show them

simply kissing, so the tingly nature of their joint spell work had to fill in the rest.

In 2018, teen witches made a comeback when Sabrina returned to TV in the much bloodier *Chilling Adventures of Sabrina*, which ran through 2020. In this

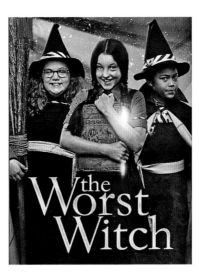

racy reimagining, Sabrina (Kiernan Shipka) still lives with her aunts and juggles mortal and witch high school drama, but also battles the forces of evil and Satan himself. Twenty years post-*Buffy*, the show's exploration of sexuality was much less coy and features a number of queer characters. Sabrina's cousin Ambrose (Chance Perdomo), for example, is pansexual, and classmate Theo (Lachlan Watson) is transgender.

"Sabrina is active in fighting for justice," Shipka, who describes Sabrina as a "woke witch," has said. "She's passionate about giving people the rights they deserve."

In *Motherland: Fort Salem*, a female witch's power is so explicitly linked to her sexual maturity that her "mark of the witch" becomes "sparkly" when she loses her virginity. The series takes place in an alternate reality where the persecution of the Salem witches was halted in the 1600s when they agreed to serve in the U.S. military. For more than 300 years, descendants of witches—including series leads Raelle (Taylor Hickson), Tally (Jessica Sutton) and Abigail (Ashley Nicole Williams)—are conscripted on their 18th birthdays and begin basic training in combat magic. Initially at odds, the three cadets' growing bond sees them through as respected adults and trusted institutions prove complex and morally ambiguous.   —*Jules Wilkinson*

CASSANDRA
PETERSON AS
ELVIRA

ENTICING ENCHANTRESSES

There's no shortage of on-screen sirens who use their sex appeal as part of their sorcery, but it's mostly on their own terms.

KIM NOVAK
IN *BELL, BOOK AND CANDLE*

VERONICA LAKE
IN *I MARRIED A WITCH*

ELIZABETH MONTGOMERY
IN *BEWITCHED*

173

Anyone who's ever set foot in a costume store around Halloween knows there are roughly 50,000 variations of the "sexy" witch costume with low-cut or skintight black frocks and fishnets. It's enough to make one think modern witches derive their power from their cleavage.

But according to Daniel Gifford, PhD, the hot witch getup actually dates back to the beginning of the 20th century, when women began taking a more active role in their lives and romances. "The witch is a woman who has power—the power to create spells, alter fate and change the future," he writes on smithsonian.com. "The witch *does*; the witch doesn't wait. And for many women of the era, this was an attractive aspect of the witch, with one obvious problem: What young, self-actualizing woman wants to see herself as an old hag? This is why the motif of the beautiful witch gained such

popular currency. The beautiful witch had both power and attractiveness, and could use both to make her own decisions about romance, suitors and the future."

Not surprisingly, pop culture is packed with sexy sorceresses, but a good chunk of these characters hold true to those strong, independent roots from the early 20th century. Far more often than their mortal counterparts, these beautiful witches drive their stories' action.

WITCHY BLOND WIVES

In 1942's *I Married a Witch*, Veronica Lake is certainly take-charge as Jennifer, a Salem-era witch who vows to make life miserable for the descendants of the man who burned her at the stake. When her spirit is reawakened, she finds said descendant in aspiring politician Wallace Wooley (Fredric March), and tries to give him a love potion so he'll fall for her and she can "make him suffer, body and soul!" Of course, things go epically awry and she falls for him. Still, as Yohana Desta wrote in *Vanity Fair* on the flick's 75th anniversary: "Lake holds and drives the picture, rather than March. He's plenty charming, but stiff by comparison."

Fellow blond stunner Kim Novak also uses a little magic in the 1958 rom-com *Bell, Book*

SANDRA BULLOCK IN *PRACTICAL MAGIC*

NICOLE KIDMAN IN *PRACTICAL MAGIC*

HOLLY MARIE COMBS, SHANNEN DOHERTY AND ALYSSA MILANO IN *CHARMED*

and Candle. As free-spirited Greenwich Village witch Gillian, she casts a love spell on her book-publisher neighbor Shepherd (Jimmy Stewart) in an attempt to get back at his fiancée (Janice Rule), who was Gillian's enemy at Wellesley. Once again hilarity and love ensue, but Novak's character is hardly a cookie cutter of '50s femininity. "She brings a unique independence to the role of Gillian," Kimberly Pierce wrote for Geek Girl Authority. "As Shepherd falls deeper into her spell, there's almost a traditional-gender-role reversal between the characters." At one point, when Shep is pressuring her to marry, Gillian actually quips. "Shep, that's the woman's remark usually."

Bewitched creator Sol Saks has said both films were hefty influences for his hit 1964–1972

> **"ELVIRA KIND OF REPRESENTS ALL THE PEOPLE WHO DON'T FIT IN.... SHE'S KIND OF AN OUTCAST, BUT SHE DOESN'T CARE. I THINK IT GIVES PEOPLE LIKE THAT THE ATTITUDE OF, 'I DON'T HAVE TO BE SO UPSET ABOUT IT. I CAN JUST GO MY OWN WAY AND BE WHO I AM.'"**
>
> — *Actress Cassandra Peterson*

sitcom. Like Novak and Lake, Elizabeth Montgomery is golden-haired and gorgeous as Samantha Stephens, a witch who can work her magic—turning an ape into a male model, or summoning snacks—with a twitch of her pert nose. More often than not, it was Sam who saved husband Darrin (Dick York and, later, Dick Sargent), even if to outsiders, like Darrin's boss, she appeared the perfect suburban homemaker.

"The underlying feminism of *Bewitched* revealed a 'typical housewife' who is actually more powerful than her husband," writes Linda Napikoski for thoughtexchange.com. "Samantha used her witchcraft powers to solve all sorts of problems, despite having promised her husband that she would no longer practice magic."

CARICE VAN HOUTEN IN *GAME OF THRONES*

MELONIE DIAZ, MADELEINE MANTOCK AND SARAH JEFFERY IN THE *CHARMED* REBOOT

175

OVERT & UNAPOLOGETIC

In the 1980s, Cassandra Peterson poured killer curves into a gown with an impressively plunging neckline to host horror films as Elvira on L.A.'s KHJ–TV. The character became a cult phenomenon, spawning the 1988 comedy *Elvira, Mistress of the Dark*. B-list by design, the film sees Elvira quitting her job after some sexual harassment and heading to suburban Massachusetts, where she gets serious shade from the uptight citizenry. Being true to herself, however, is what ultimately saves the day.

Despite Elvira's overt sexuality and innuendo-driven humor, Peterson says her biggest fans aren't lusty lads. "I hear so much from women and girls that growing up Elvira was a huge hero for them, because…she's going to do what she wants to do, and she's not going to put up with any B.S. from guys," Peterson told *LA Magazine*. Still, after 40 years, the actress admits she sometimes wishes for a different costume, "something much more comfortable…a muumuu and flip-flops."

The mid-'80s also saw three of the world's most beautiful and bankable actresses—Cher, Michelle Pfeiffer and Susan Sarandon—get their hex on in *The Witches of Eastwick*. The link between sex and the craft is hardly subtle; the trio of small-town pals each get hot and heavy with devilish stranger Daryl Van Horne (Jack Nicholson) and thus uncover their collective powers. Based loosely on John Updike's novel, the film was a huge hit, although not with some practicing witches, who saw it as "anti-witch" or a cautionary tale.

A decade later in 1998, Sandra Bullock and Nicole Kidman starred as spell-casting sisters Sally and Gillian in *Practical Magic* (Kidman crafted out again in *Bewitched*, a 2005 flick inspired by the TV show). The film certainly didn't hide its stars' ravishing good looks and, as far as the story, we'll just say this wasn't how these ladies won their Oscars. Refreshingly, though, the movie refuses to pit women against each other. In the climax, Sally needs help from other townswomen who'd always judged her. Lo and behold, they were just curious. As Aunt Jet (Dianne Wiest) says: "There's a little witch in all of us."

That same year, Shannen Doherty, Holly Marie Combs and Alyssa Milano started harnessing the power of three to save the world as the Halliwell sisters on

ANGELA BASSETT IN *AHS: COVEN*

> ### "I LOVE THAT MOVIE [PRACTICAL MAGIC]… WE'RE REALLY GOOD SISTERS."
>
> *Sandra Bullock on Nicole Kidman*

TV's *Charmed*. Milano called it the "perfect postfeminist girl-power" show, as Prue, Piper and Phoebe dealt with real-world challenges as well as demons, devils and the like. But its nearly all-white cast hardly challenged ideals of beauty. "All of the women are fit and young with the exception of Grams, who is fit, but older," Princess Weekes writes at the Mary Sue website, adding outfits got skimpier after Doherty's character was killed and Rose McGowan joined as long-lost half sister Paige. "After the fourth season, it feels like a race to put Alyssa Milano in as little clothing as possible."

21ST-CENTURY SIRENS

A 2018 reboot of the series cast a diverse group of stars—Madeleine Mantock, Melonie Diaz and Sarah Jeffery—as half sisters (same mother; different fathers) who discover they're the world's most powerful witches. The series was recently green-lit for another season, despite criticism from the original stars, who weren't consulted, and some mixed reviews. "The writing has a clumsy, faux-feminist political bent that undercuts the show's desire to provide an empowering message about female power," claims vulture.com.

Game of Thrones' "Red Witch" Melisandre (Carice van Houten) used magic to maintain a pretty facade, and more than one of her spells involved seduction. She made some very, very suspect choices (backing Stannis, burning Shireen!), but remained one of the series' most powerful characters.

American Horror Story: Coven made a sort of reverse link to sex in 2013, when teen Zoe (Taissa Farmiga) discovers she's a witch and her power will cause a lover to die during the deed. Much of the series took place at a supernatural New Orleans boarding school, and there were indeed several sexy sorceresses. But there were also juicy parts for nonhag older and middle-aged women, including Kathy Bates, Jessica Lange, Sarah Paulson and Frances Conroy. With so few Black witches in TV and film, it was exciting to see Gabourey Sidibe as Queenie and Angela Bassett as Marie Laveau. But where the real Laveau (see page 50) was a healer known to bring groups together, the show's version makes Laveau a baby-sacrificing antagonist.

But like her sexy-witch sistren, she is controlling the action, and looking good doing it!

CHER, SUSAN SARANDON AND MICHELLE PFEIFFER IN *THE WITCHES OF EASTWICK*

GABOUREY SIDIBE IN *AHS: COVEN*

MALEFICENT IN DISNEY'S
SLEEPING BEAUTY

Deliciously *Devilish*

*There's something to be said for these bad-to-the-broom
witches who live on their own terms.*

The unapologetically nefarious witch, cackling as she attempts to injure the innocent, has been a staple in Hollywood since the Evil Queen dressed as an old crone and offered her stepdaughter a poisoned apple in 1937's *Snow White and the Seven Dwarfs*. Two years later, *The Wizard of Oz* painted its Wicked Witch of the West a mean green, and in *Sleeping Beauty*, Disney went so far as to give Maleficent horns and a name that literally means "doing evil." (Angelina Jolie gave the character a sympathetic retelling in 2014's *Maleficent*.)

Drawing on centuries of folklore from Russia's Baba Yaga to Grimms' fairy tales, this terrifying on-screen archetype is so embedded in our psyches from such an early age that *The Blair Witch Project* didn't even need to show the villain to terrify audiences. The 1999 flick, credited with popularizing the found-footage technique, follows amateur filmmakers (actors Heather Donahue, Michael C. Williams and Joshua Leonard, who used their real names) in their attempt to make a documentary about a supposed child-killing witch in Burkittsville, Maryland. "I had this idea of seeing a stick figure hanging from a tree and it creeped the hell out of me," co-director Daniel Myrick told *The Guardian*. Indeed, as the trio lose their way in the woods, they encounter mysterious rock formations and stick bundles, and our collective lore about the treacherous witch fills in the terror far better than any on-screen ghoul; the film made $250 million against its $60,000 budget.

"They say if you look at her you'll die from the fright of it," a similarly ill-fated would-be witch documenter says in the (much less successful) 2016 sequel *Blair Witch*. "No one who has ever seen her has lived to talk about it."

OWNING IT

Other times these bad biddies hide among us in plain sight, like Miss Eva Ernst (Anjelica Huston) in 1990's *The Witches*, based on Roald Dahl's book. At first, Eva appears as a statuesque woman and the key speaker for the Royal Society for the Prevention of Cruelty to Children. But as she addresses the convention at a seaside hotel, Eva peels back her wig and face to reveal herself as the Grand High Witch, a grotesque, taloned creature with toeless feet. Fellow conventioneers likewise show

✻ Anne Hathaway played the Grand High Witch in a 2020 remake.

✻ Anjelica Huston and her minions unveil their true child-hating form in *Witches*.

179

✳ Heather Donahue records her iconic apology monologue in *The Blair Witch Project*.

themselves, as Eva outlines her dastardly plan to turn all English children to mice.

Stories like this warn against ladies who fail to fulfill an "acceptable" feminine role. They represent the type of woman not valued by a society that has a lust for youthful lasses and occasional honor for benevolent mothers. These witches hate children and many are old and unattractive, like the cataract-eyed

gypsy in *Drag Me to Hell* or the corpulent, tentacled Ursula in *The Little Mermaid*. Yet the movies betray society's double standard, as these characters are condemned for pursuing beauty and youth, the very things that society deems would give them value.

But at least it's a gig for an actress of a certain age. "I was offered three [witch roles] when I turned 40—in one year,"

Meryl Streep told ABC News. "I thought: Oh, this is how it's gonna go?" The three-time Oscar winner did eventually play a witch, in the film adaptation of *Into the Woods*, Stephen Sondheim's subversive musical twist on fairy tales.

Conflicted messages aside, there is something appealing about owning the awful. When asked what made her Grand High Witch such a memorable character,

> **"IT WAS REALLY EASY AND I CAN'T QUITE WORK OUT WHY. MAYBE IT WAS MY REVENGE ON PEOPLE WHO HAD BEEN UNKIND TO ME AS A CHILD. BUT IT WAS VERY EASY AND A THRILL TO FREEZE UP CHILDREN."**
>
> *Actress Tilda Swinton on playing* Narnia's *White Witch*

and an icon for the LBGTQ and other marginalized communities, Huston told *Gay Vegas*, "She has fabulous powers and she revels in her ugliness and in her vileness; she's somebody who takes full advantage of being horrible."

In a 2020 remake, Anne Hathaway had a great time hamming it up in the iconic role of the Grand High Witch. Most of filming took place while she was pregnant with her second child, Jack, which had some unexpected advantages. "I was really happy on the days when my hormones were raging," she told *USA Today*. "There was no acting involved whatsoever."

The White Witch in C. S. Lewis' *The Chronicles of Narnia* isn't ugly or stereotypically black-clad, but she's about as treacherous as you can get, with her child-freezing and Aslan-slaying. And that was something Tilda Swinton loved about playing the character in the film adaptations. "This is the epitome of all evil. It's like a free pass with any kind of nonsense you can come up with," she told movieweb.com. "It doesn't have to add up. What children, in fact all of us at any age, find frightening is unreliability and emotional coldness—the idea that you

can't affect someone, that you can't see where they're coming from and [they] can change tact at any moment."

TAKING CHARGE

Such stories may be designed to terrify and reinforce stereotypes, but they also captivate and even inspire. Evil witches can be a symbol of liberation. They don't play by the narrow rules society sets for ladies. They break constraints on behavior and appearance and gender norms.

Take the trio of spell-casters in *Hocus Pocus*. Rambunctious Winnie Sanderson (Bette Midler) along with sisters Mary (Kathy Najimy) and Sarah (Sarah Jessica Parker) wreak havoc in modern Salem

after having been put to (almost) death for sucking the life from a child in the 1600s. Sure, they are ugly, broomstick (and vacuum cleaner) riders with a penchant for killing kids to retain their youth. But they dress to impress, and can belt out a tune!

Dastardly witches are often shown in opposition to innocent children like Snow White, Ariel or Dorothy, who ultimately kill them. Sometimes, however, that narrative gets flipped. In 2018 Luca Guadagnino reimagined Dario Argento's *Suspiria* from 1977, about Susie, an American attending a ballet academy in 1970s Berlin run by

THE EVIL QUEEN IN DISNEY'S *SNOW WHITE*

ANYA TAYLOR-JOY IN *THE WITCH*

TILDA SWINTON IN 2018'S *SUSPIRIA*

✣ *Hocus Pocus'*
Sanderson sisters
(Kathy Najimy, Bette
Midler and Sarah
Jessica Parker) find
their spell book.

a coven of witches. While both the original and remake are coming-of-age stories about a young woman finding agency, the movies differ in their focus. In the original, Susie kills the witches and escapes, saving herself. In Guadagnino's telling, a plot twist reveals there is no juxtaposition of the "good girl" and the evil witches. "True feminism is something that doesn't shy away from the complexity of the female identity," Guadagnino told Jezebel.

Likewise, Robert Eggers' 2015 film, *The Witch*, follows Thomasin, a young woman whose family has been banished from the 17th-century Puritan Colony over religious differences. Struggling in

an unfamiliar land, they are preyed on by all types of witches—baby-killing hags, evil seductresses, shape-shifting animals. Though innocent, Thomasin is blamed when a baby is stolen and her brothers seduced and sickened. (Spoiler alert!) Her whole family is eventually killed, and the devil—in the form of a black goat—offers Thomasin a deal to join his coven. "Wouldst thou like to live deliciously?" he asks, tempting her with butter and fine clothes.

The movie has the tagline "A New-England Folktale"—and yes, this is the type of story colonists likely used as a cautionary tale about Satan. But from another perspective, it's about a

girl struggling in a society where she has little power and her sexuality is a sin. Her Puritan life is miserable, so she chooses the way of the witch—agency and freedom. The final scene is Thomasin floating ecstatically with the coven around a bonfire. "*The Witch* may present like a highbrow horror film, but it delivers a powerful feminist message," writes *Marie Claire*'s Diane Cohen. "She's now a woman, with the awesome power to determine her own life."

Stories of wicked witches may be designed to remind women of their place, but they also show the thrill of breaking out. And who wouldn't rather live deliciously?   —*Jules Wilkinson*

❋ Meryl Streep's Witch warns of wolves and humans among the trees in *Into the Woods*.

![image](decorative triangle with crescent moon)

By the *Numbers*

Some crafty facts and figures.

1st

Rank of the *The Wizard of Oz* on Rotten Tomatoes' "100 Greatest Movies" list. The flick comes in sixth on the American Film Academy's "Greatest American Films" list.

4.6 MILLION

ESTIMATED NUMBER OF PEOPLE WHO DRESS AS A WITCH FOR HALLOWEEN—BY FAR THE MOST POPULAR COSTUME FOR ADULTS.

Number of annual Wiccan Sabbats.

50,000 *to* 60,000

Number of people put to death in Tanzania for witchcraft between 1960 and 2000. Between 2005 and 2011, 3,000 more were killed.

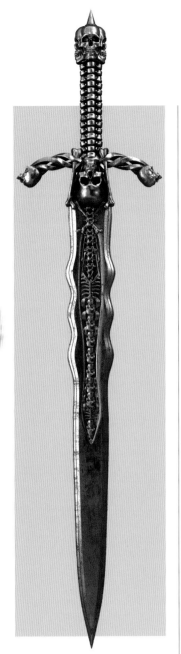

3

Number of witches in *Macbeth*.

9

Number of times they repeat their spell.

254

NUMBER OF EPISODES OF *BEWITCHED*. WITH EIGHT SEASONS (1964–1972), IT'S AMONG THE LONGEST-RUNNING FANTASY SITCOMS.

1.5 MILLION

Estimated number of practicing Wiccans and pagans in the United States.

1782

Year Anna Göldi, the last person executed for witchcraft in Europe, was decapitated in Switzerland.

78 NUMBER OF CARDS IN THE WAITE-SMITH TAROT DECK.

185

CREDITS

CENTENNIAL BOOKS

An Imprint of
Centennial Media, LLC
1111 Brickell Avenue, 10th Floor
Miami, FL 33131, U.S.A.

ISBN 978-1-951274-81-8

Distributed by
Simon & Schuster, Inc.
1230 Avenue of the Americas
New York, NY 10020, U.S.A.

For information about custom editions, special sales and premium and corporate purchases,
please contact Centennial Media at contact@centennialmedia.com.

Manufactured in China

10 9 8 7 6 5 4 3 2 1

Publishers & Co-Founders Ben Harris, Sebastian Raatz
Editorial Director Annabel Vered
Creative Director Jessica Power
Executive Editor Janet Giovanelli
Features Editor Alyssa Shaffer
Deputy Editors Ron Kelly, Anne Marie O'Connor
Managing Editor Lisa Chambers
Design Director Martin Elfers
Senior Art Director Pino Impastato
Art Directors Runyon Hall, Natali Suasnavas, Joseph Ulatowski
Copy/Production Patty Carroll, Angela Taormina
Assistant Art Director Jaclyn Loney
Senior Photo Editor Jenny Veiga
Photo Editor Keri Pruett
Production Manager Paul Rodina
Production Assistant Alyssa Swiderski
Editorial Assistant Tiana Schippa
Sales & Marketing Jeremy Nurnberg